# Strategy or Principle?

# Strategy or Principle?

The Choice between Regulation and Taxation

Mark Kelman

*Ann Arbor*

THE UNIVERSITY OF MICHIGAN PRESS

Copyright © by the University of Michigan 1999
All rights reserved
Published in the United States of America by
The University of Michigan Press
Manufactured in the United States of America
⊗ Printed on acid-free paper

2002   2001   2000   1999      4   3   2   1

*A CIP catalog record for this book is available from the British Library.*

Library of Congress Cataloging-in-Publication Data

Kelman, Mark.
    Strategy or principle? : the choice between regulation and
taxation / Mark Kelman.
        p.   cm.
    Includes bibliographical references and index.
    ISBN 0-472-11047-0 (acid-free paper)
    1. Taxation—Law and legislation—United States.   2. Fiscal
policy—United States.   I. Title.
    KF6289 .K45   1999
    343.7304—dc21                                          99-6269
                                                              CIP

*With the deepest love and gratitude to my parents,*
*Kurt and Sylvia Kelman,*
*and to the second set of parents*
*I was lucky enough to acquire as an adult,*
*my mother-in-law, Barbara Richman,*
*and the memory of my father-in-law, Bud Richman*

# Contents

# Preface

I delivered a somewhat different version of this manuscript as the forty-second annual Thomas M. Cooley Lecturer at the University of Michigan Law School in October 1997. I am especially grateful to Dean Jeffrey Lehman and the faculty at Michigan, particularly Tom Green, Sam Gross, Michael Heller, Don Herzog, Rick Hills, Saul Levmore, Kyle Logue, Catharine MacKinnon, Deborah Malamud, Bill Miller, and Julie Roin, for being generous hosts and intellectually stimulating critics of my work. I am grateful as well to workshop participants here at Stanford for their probing questions and most of all to colleagues who read and responded to earlier drafts of the manuscript: Joe Bankman, Tom Grey, Peggy Radin, and especially Barbara Fried.

I benefited greatly from the capable research assistance of Christine Wade and Lina Ericsson. Truc Do did the bulk of the research for this particular project and merits my greatest gratitude in that regard. The research was supported financially by both the Roberts Program in Law and Corporate Governance and by the Stanford Legal Research Fund, made possible by a bequest from Ira S. Lillick and by gifts from other friends of the Stanford Law School.

As always, my wonderful wife, Ann, and kids, Nick and Jake, matter most by a mile.

# CHAPTER 1

## Introduction

Governments tax their citizens and spend the resources they raise through taxation to meet a wide variety of goals.[1] Governments regulate the conduct of their citizens as well, establishing duties (conventionally described as affirmative duties) to do things the citizen would not choose to do in the absence of regulation or duties (often called negative duties) to forbear from doing things that they would otherwise spontaneously choose to do.[2] The ends that might be met through spending programs could generally be met as well through appropriately tailored regulations. At the same time, governments could almost invariably choose to spend the money raised through taxation to achieve the same goals regulatory schemes are designed to accomplish. Furthermore, citizens subject to regulation will generally have no private motive to differentiate a regulation from a tax. Their net income in a world without the regulation or the tax would be higher, so that they will experience the cost of regulatory compliance as indistinguishable from the cost of paying an explicit tax.[3]

---

1. The state's broad sorts of goals can readily be differentiated. Public finance economists traditionally speak of programs that provide public goods, correct for the misallocation of goods that occur in private markets, subsidize goods the state feels people should want (merit goods), and redistribute resources. See Richard Musgrave, *The Theory of Public Finance* (New York: McGraw-Hill, 1959), 3–22, for the classic account.

2. That the line between affirmative and negative duties may well be either unworkably blurry or just plain unhelpful in resolving questions about the propriety of imposing the duty, even if it could be drawn, is beside the point for now. Thus, whether regulations designed to protect ecosystems are described as forbidding harmful conduct or as demanding affirmative steps to preserve the environment is not, for the moment, of any concern.

3. One could classify the tax effect of regulations in a variety of ways, but I do not think the distinctions among the varieties of regulations ultimately matter to any of the arguments I explore.

A regulation may affect regulated owners' income streams either because it increases costs or because it reduces revenues. Owners may bear higher costs because they must provide costly in-kind goods on their property, expending funds out-of-pocket to comply with the regulations (e.g., an up-to-code building, workplace safety devices, a store with ramps accessible to disabled patrons). Regulations may also increase production costs without leading owners to expend funds out-of-pocket to comply with some particular mandate (e.g., a regulatory requirement to make the workplace safer might be met by slowing the production line

At times, this interchangeability or substitutability of taxation and regulation is quite transparent, and it is debated publicly whether certain regulatory mandates ought to be thought of as new taxes. Thus, for example, governments could mandate that employers purchase health insurance for some otherwise-uncovered set of employees (a regulatory mandate) or could purchase health insurance or health care for those same persons, using tax revenue (including tax revenue that might be gathered from increases in taxes on these employers). Politicians, sensitive to whether they have increased taxes or increased the deficit, might seek to characterize the employer mandate as a regulatory scheme to keep it off-budget.[4]

down). Owners may bear higher costs because regulations require providing goods in-kind off property (e.g., developer exactions to build sidewalks or parks) or buying costly goods for some particular third party or parties (e.g., mandates that employers purchase health insurance for their workers). A regulation may force an owner to forgo revenue rather than increase costs. Thus, for example, regulations that require that a small grocery store owner provide access for the disabled may not just increase out-of-pocket expenditures (e.g., the money spent building ramps) but may require him to widen aisles and carry fewer items, thus reducing sales revenue. Similarly, a zoning regulation might preclude the building of a taller or bulkier building with more rentable units; laws that prohibit selling liquor to the inebriated or cigarettes or liquor to minors deprive owners of revenue they would otherwise earn.

4. Thus, critics of President Clinton's Health Security Act of 1993, which required employers to provide coverage for all full- and part-time employees and to pay 80 percent of premium costs, subject to certain caps for small employers, deemed the employer mandates a tax. See, e.g., Jonathan Barry Forman, "The Emperor Has No Clothes: The Naked Truth Is That Health Care 'Premiums' Are Bad Taxes," *Tax Notes* 62 (1994): 1199; Paul G. Merski, "Pricing Health Care: CBO Data Show Clinton Wants $400 Billion Tax," *Wall Street Journal*, Feb. 9, 1994, A14; Meegan M. Reilly, "Employer Mandate Contested at Ways and Means Hearing," *Tax Notes* 62 (1994): 655. The Clinton administration had said that the health insurance costs would not go on budget because funds do not flow from the Treasury and are clearly earmarked for health care. See, e.g., Amy S. Cohen, "Employers' Payroll Contribution for Health Care Not a Tax, Says Gore," *Tax Notes* 61 (1993): 868. Whether the mandates constitute a tax is of no obvious moment for functionalists, but its symbolic meaning appeared enormous: as one commentator noted, "Whether the employer/employee mandate is considered as a payroll tax or a premium contribution, however, has less to do with the consequences for the federal budget and more to do with perceptions about the role and size of government" (Alexander Polinsky, "The Health Insurance Mandate: A Tax by Any Other Name?" *Tax Notes* 61 [1993]: 395).

A tax-and-spend program might involve government provision of in-kind services (the government might act as provider of health care for the medically uninsured, either by operating municipal hospitals and clinics or by contracting with for-profit or nonprofit private hospitals and clinics to provide free or below-cost care for the uninsured); government provision of cash-equivalent grants good for use in the relevant market only (the government might give vouchers to purchase health care or health insurance, as it frequently does in the food or housing markets); or government rebates for those who spend money in the relevant market. Such rebates could be awarded either through unlimited refundable tax credits or through more limited rebates for those whose tax liability is sufficient to make nonrefundable tax credits or deductions serve as cash-rebate equivalents. Thus, the government might allow

Similarly, plaintiffs in regulatory takings cases typically urge that the court direct the relevant governmental unit to accomplish its aim by substituting a tax-and-spending program that compensates the plaintiffs for the losses they will suffer if regulated. The court should not, the plaintiffs say, permit the state simply to ban development of property; instead, the court should direct the state entity to purchase a nondevelopment equitable servitude out of general funds. Similarly, plaintiffs argue that the state should not be permitted to limit the prices the plaintiffs can charge needy customers; instead, the court should force the state to give the needy customers vouchers or cash that permit them to pay market prices for the good whose price would otherwise be controlled.

At other times, this functional interchangeability may be less transparent but no less real. Regulations requiring that providers of services charge all consumers the same prices, even though the costs of providing services to some subset of consumers is higher, could be replaced by a tax-and-spend program granting direct government subsidies for those consumers who would face higher than community-rated prices in an unregulated market that sorted buyers by cost of service.[5] Conversely, many

---

all or some portion and variety of health care costs to be deductible, which would reduce purchasers' taxes by the premium price times the marginal tax rate. The government could also establish a nonrefundable tax credit at some chosen percentage of spending on the targeted good, which could be used to reduce taxes until they reached zero, or a refundable credit, which would be applied first to reducing taxes and then result in a cash rebate. The federal government helps pay for child care expenditures largely through nonrefundable tax credits, but it obviously could adopt, in whole or in part, a direct-provision method (either establishing its own free or subsidized centers or paying private businesses to operate free or below-cost centers), a regulatory method (mandating that employers provide free or subsidized day care for their employees), or a more direct cash-grant method (giving vouchers to parents to use at child care facilities).

5. See Richard Posner, "Taxation by Regulation," *Bell J. of Econ. and Mgmt. Sci.* 2 (1971): 22, for a discussion. Thus, cost-based price discrimination is often forbidden to protect some favored group (see, e.g., the protection of farmers from railroad tariffs that reflected higher marginal costs or statutes that protect smaller retailers by mandating uniform pricing by suppliers even when bulk discounts for larger retailers reflect cost differentials). But farmers could simply be paid enough to permit them to ship at unregulated prices, or smaller retailers could receive tax rebates or direct dollar subsidies to compensate for their cost disadvantage.

It is also possible to move from a regulatory system to a tax-and-spend system that benefits a broader group than those who would otherwise face higher-than-average prices. See Mark Kelman, "Health Care Rights: Distinct Claims, Distinct Justifications," *Stanford L. and Policy Rev.* 2 (1991): 90, 96–97 (discussing the advantages of levying an explicit excise tax on health insurance and redistributing the proceeds to a broad range of medically underserved citizens over proposals that would establish mandatory community rating systems for health insurance purchasers; in a mandatory community-rating system, everyone able to

traditional governmental functions now achieved through tax-and-spend methods could be replaced by regulations. Municipalities that sweep the streets and sidewalks or collect all the trash could instead require store owners to keep the areas outside their establishments clean or require property owners to take (some or all) of the garbage they generate to dumps or simply limit the amount of trash that a property owner could legally generate. Governments can vaccinate the young or require that their parents and guardians do so; the federal government can pay volunteer soldiers market-clearing wages or draft them; fire department budgets could be lowered if governments required builders to use more fire-retardant materials and/or install sprinklers and smoke alarms.

The government can also charge citizens user fees for many of the services now publicly provided (for free or at subsidized rates) or allow private parties simply to bear losses (or insure against them privately) rather than expend funds to prevent them. Once more, such choices can be transparent (adult-education courses can be provided free of charge or at cost) or more opaque (one would expect that any municipality's decision to lower spending by cutting back on the police force available to deal with residential burglaries will typically lead private homeowners to increase their own spending on precautionary protections and/or to bear, privately, higher loss levels).[6] While not identical to substituting regulatory for public tax-and-spend programs, user fees and deliberate inaction also represent alternative solutions to public policy problems.

The broad point is that there are invariably a variety of ways to meet social goals or respond to perceived social problems. Each responsive technique may generate a distinct pattern of gains and losses (and, some would argue, different levels of net gains or losses as well, at least in some cases), but alternative forms of policy responses are always available. As one illustration, take the problem of flooding. If this is a problem that some relevant governmental unit might address, it may be solved through some mixture of (a) publicly funded flood-control projects and insurance for flood victims; (b) regulations that forbid certain activities that increase

---

afford health insurance could purchase it at prices that reflect only their pro rata share of projected health costs, even if the insurer knew they were atypically risky and would thus, in an unregulated market, either refuse to serve them or demand a premium to account for additional risk).

6. For a discussion of the degree to which crime might more cost-effectively be prevented by private precautions by citizen-victims than by state punishment of offenders, see, e.g., Louis Michael Seidman, "Soldiers, Martyrs, and Criminals: Utilitarian Theory and the Problem of Crime Control," *Yale L. J.* 94 (1984): 315, 342–46.

flood risk (e.g., soil eroding conduct) or require that those in floodplains purchase private insurance at least sufficient to restore flooded property to a condition that is not detrimental to others in the community; (c) publicly operated flood-control projects paid for largely or entirely by people in the floodplains (user-fee equivalents); or (d) inaction, allowing flood loss levels to be determined by private action and flood losses dominantly to impact those who chose to build in the floodplain. There are, of course, familiar debates about the degree to which each of the alternative methods generates different levels of loss. Some claim, for instance, that public insurance leads to overbuilding in floodplains. Still others might argue that regulations generate too few benefits compared to costs, while regulatory proponents respond that they may well prescribe a more socially rational technique of net cost reduction than private parties would adopt on their own even if forced to internalize all losses because private efforts might fall prey to collective action problems leading to underinvestment in socially rational control programs. At a minimum, the different methods distribute both the costs of flooding (damage plus precautionary expenditures) and the gains from tolerating flood damage (building in floodplains) differently.

I will explore two broad questions in this book. First, in chapters 2 and 3, I consider whether and when the Constitution does (or should) limit the use of regulatory techniques and force governmental entities to substitute tax-and-spend programs for regulatory taxes.[7] More particularly, I ask when, if ever, parties subject to regulation should receive compensation, funded out of general tax revenues, for the losses engendered by the regulations.

In chapters 4 and 5, I address a second issue. Even if there are few (or no) appropriate constitutional limits on the use of regulatory taxation, what is the appropriate way to think about the practical virtues and pitfalls of regulatory taxation? It is obviously the case that not all that is constitutional is prudent. In this essay, I tend to emphasize some of the advantages regulatory strategies may have over tax-and-spend programs in certain set-

---

7. In addressing this question, I will also attempt to answer a question that litigants do not appear to have asked: might taxpayers have a valid constitutional complaint against the use of tax-and-spend programs that would permit taxpayers to demand that the relevant government entity substitute a regulatory scheme, a user fee, or inaction (letting losses lie) for taxing and spending? I will argue that the fact that taxpayers clearly do not have such a complaint under current jurisprudential standards bears on but hardly settles the question of whether plaintiffs ought to be able to force governments to move toward tax-and-spend programs.

tings, though I will try not to slight the more widely heard arguments against the practice.[8] I do so largely because the affirmative case for regulatory taxation has been, in my view, understated.

In keeping with this book's basic conceptual organizing theme—that regulatory taxation closely resembles taxing and spending—I will divide the discussion of the virtues and flaws of regulatory taxation into two broad parts. I will look at arguments emphasizing why regulatory taxation might in some circumstances be a superior and in some circumstances an inferior form of taxation (implicit revenue raising). I will also discuss why regulatory taxation might in some circumstances be an effective and in others an ineffective method of service provision (implicit spending).

In chapter 5, I also address political-process arguments that legislatures will make better decisions if forced to raise and allocate funds more explicitly. In discussing process, I express considerable skepticism about the argument most frequently articulated by those wary of the use of regulation—that the aggregate costs and the identity of the beneficiaries of regulation are unduly hidden. Instead, my chief worry is that the beneficiaries of regulation have illegitimately sheltered these programs from cost-benefit scrutiny on the grounds that regulation, conventionally, is thought to be designed solely to prevent rights infringements rather than to (implicitly) tax and deliver services more efficaciously and on the grounds that there is a duty not to calculate the costs and benefits of avoiding such infringements.

---

8. I by no means believe that regulation is typically superior to explicit tax-and-transfer programs: on the contrary, I have frequently chastised attempts to distribute income to particular favored beneficiary classes through antidiscrimination regulations rather than to distribute through tax-and-spend programs to those defined in terms of their individual need rather than their group status. In a wide array of situations, I believe that progressive taxation followed by explicit legislative budgeting of funds is superior to regulatory options. See, e.g., Mark Kelman and Gillian Lester, *Jumping the Queue: An Inquiry into the Legal Treatment of Students with Learning Disabilities* (Cambridge: Harvard University Press, 1997), chap. 8; Mark Kelman, "Alternative Concepts of Discrimination in 'General Ability' Job Testing," *Harvard L. Rev.* 104 (1991): 1158, 1183–94; Mark Kelman, "Health Care Rights."

# CHAPTER 2

# Current Constitutional Practice

## A Preview of the Constitutional Arguments

In this chapter, I will detail my view of current takings doctrine. In chapter 3, I construct and then attack what I view as the strongest case for a more interventionist takings law that would demand that owners receive compensation when they must comply with costly regulatory mandates in a substantially broader range of cases than the Supreme Court would today.

The review of doctrine in this chapter will not be dominantly normative, though I will note some of what strike me as especially peculiar features of existing case law. Instead, this chapter largely describes how I believe today's Supreme Court would likely deal with owners' claims that a governmental entity may not impose simple regulatory mandates but must instead substitute some sort of tax-and-spend program that relieved the owners of the costs of regulatory compliance. The Court could direct that the state entity relieve these burdens either by banning the regulatory scheme altogether or, more plausibly, by directing that the owners be compensated for bearing compliance costs.

In discussing both the constitutional issues in the next two chapters and the prudential ones thereafter, I will quite frequently refer to the requirement under Title III of the Americans with Disabilities Act (ADA)[1] that public accommodation owners must take reasonable steps to insure that their places of business are accessible to people with disabilities without charging disabled customers any of the incremental or fixed costs of accommodation. Accommodation under the ADA is usually thought of as design accommodations that store owners are required to provide for the mobility impaired.[2] At least insofar as the issue is prospective design deci-

---

1. 42 U.S.C. §§12182 et seq. See also 28 C.F.R. pt. 36 (regulations construing Title III).

2. In such cases, the cost of accommodation, if positive at all, is typically a one-time fixed cost (e.g., the installation of ramps), and a marginal-cost pricer would not charge a positive price to any particular mobility-impaired customer. Questions about the appropriate allocation of the average cost to insure that the feature was built would certainly be important, however.

sions rather than retrofitting, though, public accommodation owners often bear no cost at all in these cases. Instead, they must simply rethink the way in which buildings are designed. Ramps may cost no more than stairs to install in new buildings, and though they may initially be unfamiliar to at least some nondisabled patrons, customer adjustment may be rapid.[3]

But there are certainly cases covered by the ADA in which the incremental cost of accommodation is indisputably positive, and it is lucid that public accommodation owners must still bear the cost as long as it is reasonable. For example, a doctor or lawyer serving a severely hearing-impaired client must, under prevailing interpretations of the ADA, provide someone to facilitate communication between the client and the lawyer if the lawyer cannot sign, without charging the client the cost of hiring a sign interpreter unless there were alternative, effective means of communication.[4]

The ADA example is an especially apt one to explore, even though, for reasons I will detail, there is no realistic chance that the Supreme Court would interfere with the federal government's substantive goal of increasing inclusiveness for those with disabilities either by forbidding regulations of public accommodation owners that require greater inclusiveness or by ordering that owners be compensated for the costs of increasing inclusion. First, though, it is a useful example even in regard to the takings discussion. Conceptually, it is surely the case that insofar as the ADA demands that private actors provide beneficial, non-market-rational treatment to certain customers (or workers),[5] it could be said to function as a broad-gauged redistributive social program, designed to funnel social resources

---

3. Assuming that there are positive costs for those who must retrofit that would not be present if the owner had anticipated, before building, the needs of those with impaired mobility, one still might argue that these costs were engendered by the prior failure to account for the interests of those with impaired mobility. In this sense, some would argue that owners bear positive costs only when they must remedy their own prior negligence or bigotry.

4. See, e.g., *Nat'l. Disability L. Reptr.* 4 (1993): 159; *Nat'l. Disability L. Reptr.* 5 (1993): 142 (DOJ informs physicians that they must insure that there is effective communication with the patient, though there is no single proscribed means of communication: "A physician may not impose a surcharge on any particular individual with a disability to cover the cost of measures, such as providing auxiliary aids, that are required by the ADA."); *Mayberry v. Von Valtier,* 843 F. Supp. 1160 (E.D. Mich. 1994) (defendant cannot be granted summary judgment in suit where she protests obligation to provide medical services to plaintiff though she loses money when she does so, given the need to pay $28.00 for an interpreter when her net receipts for the patient visit are only $13.94).

5. The distinction between traditional antidiscrimination norms, which demand no more than impersonal market-rational treatment of customers and workers, and the more politically progressive views of the antidiscrimination norm embodied in the ADA's requirement

to a class of deserving beneficiaries. Such redistribution, though, should arguably be funded not by the narrow subset of public accommodation owners (or employers) who happen to deal directly with the beneficiary class but by the taxpaying public generally. Second, in terms of the prudential concerns, the ADA's inclusiveness mandates raise all three of the basic conceptual issues one must confront in evaluating the propriety of the regulatory tax. To what extent is an implicit tax on public accommodation owners a good one? To what extent is the implicit spending program enacted by the statute in which private parties bear the costs of providing accommodation services superior to alternative state-based spending programs designed to increase the ability of those with disabilities to participate in the marketplace? Finally, to what degree is the political process distorted by having a subset of private parties rather than the state bear the costs of providing accommodation services?

There seem to me to be two interpretations of the Takings Clause[6] that would demand that the Court invalidate a considerably broader range of uncompensated regulations than it now does. The second of these interpretations will be the subject of chapter 3. The first of these interpretations is a libertarian one. In such a theory, any individual or group of individuals, no matter how large, must be immunized from any losses, whether a result of regulation or explicit taxation, if the regulatory or tax program diminishes the income the individual or individuals would have privately appropriated and controlled in a world in which the state did no more than protect some real (or imagined) common law (or natural) property, tort, and contract rights, and tax the individuals to provide a small set of legitimate public goods (police protection, contract enforcement).[7]

---

that sellers and employers make reasonable, positive cost accommodations to customers and workers with disabilities, requiring non-market-rational treatment when market-rational treatment is deemed unduly exclusionary, is the main theme in Kelman and Lester, *Jumping the Queue*, 199–213. Impersonal market-rational sellers treat customers as nothing more or less than sources of revenue, net of the costs of service, and care nothing about personal attributes, including ascriptive status; impersonal market-rational employers treats workers as nothing but embodied net marginal products.

6. The Fifth Amendment reads, in relevant part, "nor shall private property be taken for public use, without just compensation." The Fifth Amendment was first applied to the states by virtue of the Fourteenth Amendment in *Chicago, B. and Q. R. Co. v. Chicago,* 166 U.S. 226 (1897).

7. It is beside the point for now that the gains from the traditional "night watchman's state" functions are hardly evenly distributed among citizens: police must be deployed in particular ways, and the methods will redound more to the benefit of some potential victims than others; state subsidies for contract-enforcing courts help actual and potential disputants more than others; those more vulnerable to "force or fraud" are aided more by a state vigilant in preventing them.

I do not address libertarianism directly in this book, however. I largely ignore libertarian theories of the Takings Clause for three reasons, the last of which is most significant: First, I strongly suspect there is no realistic chance that today's Court would be tempted to adopt a libertarian outlook. It is not realistic to believe that the Court might reject redistributive taxation or cut all taxes that fund programs that do not provide traditional public goods. Nor will the Court forbid states from abating undesirable conduct that the common law of nuisance would have permitted.

Second, I have addressed what I take to be the moral and intellectual emptiness of libertarianism on many occasions in the past and see little reason to repeat or even mildly refine arguments that I have already made.[8] To the degree that some quasi-libertarians derive libertarian con-

---

8. See, e.g., Mark Kelman, *A Guide to Critical Legal Studies* (Cambridge: Harvard University Press, 1987); Mark Kelman, "A Critique of Conservative Legal Thought," in *The Politics of Law,* ed. D. Kairys, 2d ed. (New York: Pantheon Books, 1990), 436; Mark Kelman, "Taking *Takings* Seriously: An Essay for Centrists," *California L. Rev.* 74 (1986): 1829; Mark Kelman, "The Necessary Myth of Objective Causation Judgments in Liberal Political Theory," *Chicago-Kent L. Rev.* 63 (1987): 579. Essentially, the main arguments are as follows: (a) Libertarians inadequately acknowledge the deepest legal realist insight, ultimately refined and revised "economistically" by Coase, that entitlements are invariably set in situations in which parties make competing claims to the same resource and that the collective choice to favor one claimant over another must be grounded in consequentialist reasoning about the impact of favoring one class of claimants over another. Thus, it is inevitable that rights to exclude interfere with rights to access, that protecting monopolistic control over intellectual property interferes with freer use, and that expanding use rights for property owners interferes with neighbors' immunity from nuisancelike damages. Decisions to favor one or the other competing claimants follow no natural law order but involve the resolution of ordinary political policy disputes. (b) Libertarians inadequately acknowledge the impossibility of defining coercive behavior without reference to a predefined entitlement framework, believing wrongly that one can define a just natural-rights entitlement scheme as one in which people are free to do anything but coerce others, failing to recognize that one cannot define when one is acting coercively unless an entitlement scheme is already in place. Thus, it is transparently the case that an agreement to pay money to avoid being drowned is a product of illegitimate duress, but one cannot tell whether a contract to pay to have one's life saved is a product of duress without resolving the prior question of whether the lifesaver has a preexisting duty to save. (c) Libertarians are ill-advised to reason about the proper scope of the state by imagining that the state's conduct is permissible only if it enacts programs that simply collectivize the performance of duties individuals have in their dyadic relationships with one another. For example, the fact that one may believe that there are reasonable arguments why an individual may owe no duty of charitable beneficence to other discrete individuals in need (e.g., because such duties are hard to define in rulelike form or because they are not fully realizable in the sense that no individual could meet demands to alleviate all arguably similarly situated need) explains nothing about whether it is legitimate for the state to establish mandatory beneficent tax-and-spend programs to aid the needy: the duties the state imposes on individuals to pay redistributive taxes can, for example, be framed in quite rulelike form,

clusions less from a belief that there is some defined set of natural rights than a belief that any state that does not act as if there were such a set of defined rights will be subject to a nightmare of unproductive rent seeking by organized constituencies seeking to enrich themselves through politics rather than production, I have addressed some of these claims as well.[9]

Finally, and most important, libertarianism is as hostile, at the theoretical level, to broad-based taxes coupled with spending programs as it is to regulation and hence does not really attempt to address the precise problem I am dealing with in this book, the effort to force governmental entities to choose to tax and spend rather than to regulate. Richard Epstein, the most prominent modern proponent of a libertarian view of the Takings Clause, is, as a pragmatic matter, more tolerant of broad-based progressive tax-and-transfer programs than any other forms of government activity beyond the minimal state.[10] But he still believes that redistributive welfare transfers, even if broadly funded, are illegitimate as a matter of principle and should be invalidated by the Court except for the reliance interests their beneficiaries have built up over the past half century.[11]

Instead, I will, in chapter 3, describe what I believe to be the most plausible constitutional argument for a theory of judicial review of regulations that would be more activist than current jurisprudence—i.e., a theory that would lead the Court to demand compensation be paid to those whose income was adversely affected by a regulatory program in many more cases than I believe today's Court would.[12] Essentially, the activist argument that I will detail has three broad parts.

---

and both the individual's duty to pay such taxes and the collectivity's capacity to fully meet need are fully realizable.

9. See Mark Kelman, "On Democracy-Bashing: A Skeptical Look at the Theoretical and 'Empirical' Practice of the Public Choice Movement," *Virginia L. Rev.* 74 (1988): 199, 236–68 (arguing that the empirical evidence that a variety of seemingly public-interested programs are in fact ineffectual in meeting legitimate, public-regarding ends but are effective only to meet the ends of powerful, organized constituencies is paltry and persuasive only to those strongly ideologically predisposed to the conclusion).

10. See, e.g., Richard Epstein, "A Last Word on Eminent Domain," *U. of Miami L. Rev.* 41 (1986): 253, 272–75.

11. See Richard Epstein, *Takings: Private Property and the Power of Eminent Domain* (Cambridge: Harvard University Press, 1985), 314–27.

12. The case I construct is inspired by my reading of Justice Scalia's dissenting opinion in *Pennell v. City of San Jose,* 485 U.S. 1, 15 (1988) (Scalia, J., concurring in part and dissenting in part), and his majority opinion in *Nollan v. California Coastal Commission,* 483 U.S. 825 (1987), as well as by some of the language in Justice Rehnquist's majority opinion in *Dolan v. City of Tigard,* 512 U.S. 374 (1994). When I describe this as the "most persuasive" argument

First, proponents of this view, unlike libertarians, feel that the government is permitted great latitude in enacting broad-based traditional taxes (e.g., on income, consumption generally, consumption of particular commodities, property) and in spending these tax proceeds. Thus, on the taxation side, there is no natural, constitutionalized right to hold on to one's market wages or investment returns or to pay market-level commodity prices rather than prices that include explicit or implicit excise taxes. On the spending side, there are no significant limits on either the implicit or explicit spending power.[13]

Second, again distinct from libertarians, proponents of this view argue that the Court should be extremely deferential to regulation, despite its negative taxlike effects on the regulated party, as long as a challenged regulation at least arguably serves to rectify a market failure. A governmental entity's claim that it is correcting market failure should be heard extremely sympathetically. This belief holds true if the government seeks to stop the regulated actor from (helping to) generate a social cost or seeks to allocate a social cost to one of two responsible parties. Even if the regulated party is not causing harm in some moralistic or tortlike sense,[14] the relevant point is that the regulated party and the beneficiary of the regulation interact in such a way that social costs are generated by their interaction: that is to say, the hypothetical sum of the value of their two ventures in isolation from one another is higher than the sum of their values given their interaction. The state entity's claim should also be heard sympathetically if it claims its regulation prevents sellers from exploiting buyers as a

---

I can construct, what I mean to say is both (a) that, as a predictive matter, the Court is most likely to adopt this argument if it adopts any substantially more interventionist approach, and (b) I believe this argument is most worthy of serious normative consideration, in the sense that it is (at least minimally) formally realizable, consistent with past case law, and grounded in the sort of genuine substantive concern with fairness and political process that should animate a constitutional theory of the Takings Clause. It is, nonetheless, ultimately quite unpersuasive in my view.

13. Thus, the Court is not expected either to put teeth into the currently hyperdeferential public use/public purpose limits on the exercise of the eminent domain power or to subject all spending programs to an invigorated public use limitation.

14. The relevant line in determining the legitimacy of the regulation is certainly not the traditional malfeasance-nonfeasance line, which Scalia explicitly disclaims in *Lucas v. South Carolina Coastal Council,* 505 U.S. 1003, 1024–26 (1992). Even inaction will be deemed legitimately regulable as long as mandating changes in the regulated party's conduct would have a greater impact on third parties than would mandated shifts in the conduct of other citizens not forced to bear the cost of regulation.

result of consumer misinformation, some variety of monopoly power, or duress (once more, all quite broadly understood).[15]

What makes this theory less deferential than current takings jurisprudence to the government's decision to proceed through regulation? The third, and critical, point is that the Court will demand compensation for owners whose property declines in value as a result of any regulation that benefits others at the expense of the regulated party rather than avoids what a deferential court might think of as some form of harm growing out of the atypical, interactive relationship between the regulated party and the parties aided by the regulation. The Court may well be extremely deferential in deciding that regulated parties would, in the absence of regulation, worsen the position of some other party with whom they interact or exploit the regulation's beneficiaries under some theory or other of illegitimate contracting, but if the Court decides that there is nothing resembling this sort of quasi-tort or an (arguably) unjust contract, the regulation must be supplanted by a tax-and-spend program.

**Current Practice: An Overview**

Any interpretation of the Court's current takings jurisprudence will inevitably be both idiosyncratic and incomplete. Though I purport to do

---

15. There is one exception to this principle, carried over from current Supreme Court practice. Where the regulation renders the owner's property fundamentally valueless, the state will owe the owner compensation even though it might colorably claim that the regulation reduces or allocates a social cost, unless the regulation abates something that would be adjudged a nuisance under either traditional nuisance law in the relevant jurisdiction or some modest reinterpretation of historical nuisance law consistent with common law incrementalism. This is my view of the holding in *Lucas.* But in other regulation cases, the court will not require that the legislature track either the common law or libertarian interpretations of it. The legislature can, for example, protect underinformed consumers who have not been victims of fraud, conventionally understood.

The Court could theoretically, even if following this generally deferential theory, be somewhat stricter in scrutinizing whether beneficiaries of the regulation are adequately publicly dispersed than it would be in scrutinizing whether beneficiaries of an explicit spending program are adequately publicly dispersed, though it is not clear that the complaining property owners care a great deal about the spending side of the equation or that the theory really does demand stricter review of implicit spending than the remarkably modest scrutiny usually seen for explicit spending. The key case embodying the viewpoint that the courts ought to scrutinize the implicit spending in regulatory programs far more carefully than they would scrutinize a legislature's explicit expenditures is Judge Kozinski's opinion in *Hall v. City of Santa Barbara,* 833 F. 2d 1270 (9th Cir. 1987), *cert. denied* 485 U.S. 940 (1988), a case whose reasoning the Supreme Court failed to adopt in *Yee v. City of Escondido,* 503 U.S. 519 (1992).

little more than give as straightforward and impartial a description of current practice in this section as I can, I am aware that all the relevant texts can be read in many ways and that I read them in very few. I am also aware that some might view it as necessary, or at least most profitable, to describe current practice in terms of the broad animating principles from which particular results derive, believing, quite reasonably, that it is ordinarily difficult to understand legal rules without regard to the purposes that motivate them. I do not think, though, that current takings doctrine really meets any articulable goal or even a relatively small number of competing or skew goals.[16] Nonetheless, it is not so chaotic that one cannot do a reasonable job predicting results. Instead, the Court seems to identify certain features of litigated cases that are treated as salient for decision purposes and then declares how it will deal with all those cases possessing these features. While cases characterized as having a particular decisive feature could be characterized instead as having some different salient feature, dictating a different outcome, there appears to me to be enough consensus among the justices in characterizing the features of the cases to permit us to anticipate how a case will be classified.

---

16. A number of scholars do believe that takings jurisprudence can be rationalized. Still others believe either that it represents an uneasy compromise between alternative visions or that it could be rationalized if principles distinct from those in use were adopted. I do not intend in this piece to criticize or endorse any of these more global theories of the Takings Clause. Many writers believe that practice can be explained on the basis of a single principle. See, e.g., Frank Michelman, "Property, Utility, and Fairness: Comments on the Ethical Foundations of 'Just Compensation' Law," *Harvard L. Rev.* 80 (1967): 1165 (existing practice can indeed be explained on utilitarian grounds, takings do and should occur when the benefits of the taking outweigh the costs, and compensation is and should be paid in those circumstances when the demoralization costs of not compensating an owner outweigh the administrative costs of compensating); Andrea Peterson, "The Takings Clause: In Search of Underlying Principles, Part II—Takings as Intentional Deprivations of Property without Moral Justification," *California L. Rev.* 78 (1990): 55 (courts do and should find a compensable taking when the government forces claimants to give up their property, whether through regulation, physical action, or formal condemnation, unless the government entity is seeking to prevent or punish conduct—or failure to act—that the community would consider wrongful). Many other writers believe that existing practice draws on a small number of competing currents. See, e.g., Bruce Ackerman, *Private Property and the Constitution* (New Haven: Yale University Press, 1977) (courts oscillate between a lay, physicalist conception of property and a "scientific policymaker view" that focuses more on the value of ownership rights in deciding when property has been taken). For an example of a work suggesting the desirability of developing a takings law distinct from the present one and embodying a single principle, see Epstein, *Takings* (any time a citizen's distributive share is lower as a result of identifiable government conduct than it would have been had the government done no more than enforce something akin to Lockean/common law entitlements, a per se taking has occurred, and explicit compensation must be given unless the citizen has already received implicit in-kind compensation).

Takings cases currently fall into one of four basic patterns—that is, a case will be deemed to have one of four salient features. First, the court may find that the governmental entity has seized a traditional property interest (e.g., a fee, an easement, the right to devise a beneficial interest in land) by taking the title itself for its own use, permanently physically occupying the property or some portion thereof, granting a traditional interest to a third party or parties, or simply destroying the interest.[17] These title seizures are per se compensable takings. If the government's action is so characterized, the government will owe the owner compensation. The Court will not engage in any balancing tests in which it looks at whether the owner lost too much under the facts and circumstances of the particular case before deciding that the owner must be paid.

Second, an owner may claim that the governmental entity has applied regulations that so limit the owner's ordinary use rights that the property is rendered essentially valueless. To decide this sort of case, the Court must first decide that the owner has not illegitimately disaggregated the property, either physically or conceptually, into unduly small parcels or unduly small legal rights whose value is virtually eliminated by the challenged regulation. If, though, the state has rendered all of some properly aggregated property valueless, the Court will typically demand that the state compensate the owner for this complete destruction of value. The state could avoid this ordinary obligation to compensate only by showing that the regulation that rendered the property virtually valueless abates what the regulating jurisdiction's courts would historically have called a nuisance or might have called a nuisance under emerging nuisance law.

Third, an owner may claim that a regulation imposes too great a cost. To sustain this claim, the owner must first show that the property's value declines by some (imprecisely defined) substantial amount as a result of the regulatory scheme. (The question of whether property declines substantially in value depends in part on whether owners derive reciprocal benefits from the regulation beyond those that ordinary citizens would derive; if owners derive such benefits, the net decline in the property's value, which is the relevant decline that results from the presence of the regulatory scheme, will be lower than the difference in the value of the property alone, unregulated, and its value subject to the regulation in

---

17. It is somewhat more conventional, and not at all objectionable from my viewpoint, to say that this first class of cases consists of those in which the Court decides *either* that title was seized or that possession was taken through a permanent physical invasion. I treat the sorts of permanent physical invasions that the Court declares to be per se takings as a method of seizing title.

question. Thus, for example, a single property owner might benefit a great deal if her property were freed from zoning restrictions, but the benefit would be wiped out if all similarly situated properties were similarly exempted, and she bore the negative externalities of imprudent, unregulated land use. In such a case, the property does not decline in value as a result of the regulation.)[18] If the regulation interferes with legitimate investment-backed expectations, the owner may well be entitled to compensation, depending on the purposes the government's regulatory scheme serves.

Fourth, developers may claim that they are subject to an illicit exaction.[19] Read narrowly, as I will read them in this chapter on current practice,[20] the Court's two recent exaction cases (*Nollan* and *Dolan*) simply give lower courts guidance about how to sort out whether the relevant state entity has engaged in a per se taking of a traditional property interest or whether its conduct should be reviewed, more deferentially, as a regulation even though the developer has had to surrender title to some portion of its property. The problem (in the Court's view) posed by the exactions cases the Court has decided is as follows: Normally, if a governmental entity bans development outright, the ban would be reviewed under the third standard just described—that is, the owner would be entitled to compensation only if the development ban caused some unduly substantial

---

18. The challenged regulatory scheme most typically would limit common law use rights—for example, prohibitions on altering historical-landmark-status buildings or laws increasing duties to prevent lateral subsidence. But such a plan might also limit exclusion rights (e.g., a scheme demanding that political speakers have access to shopping center property or that public accommodations serve people in a nondiscriminatory fashion) or disposition rights (e.g., a scheme forbidding eviction of tenants without just cause or prohibiting a mobile-home-park landlord from rejecting a tenant's purchaser as a new tenant). Price controls would interfere with something that could be described as either use or disposition rights.

19. In typical exaction cases, developers are denied building permits by the relevant local governments unless some land, good, service, or money is provided. In some sense, though, most regulatory cases could be described as exaction cases: for example, the ADA case on which I often focus could be seen as an exaction case, particularly if the ADA is imagined as applying only prospectively. In exchange for permission to open a place of public accommodations, the developer must provide, for example, ramps that make the building more accessible to people with mobility impairments. (At the same time, of course, the ADA could be seen to establish a simple building code, regulating the features of acceptable buildings.) Similarly, shopping-center owners might say that they have to dedicate a portion of their center to use by speakers in order to open. However, the Court characterizes cases as exaction cases only when developers lose title control over some portion of what would otherwise be their property in exchange for permission to build.

20. This first reading is basically most consistent with, though not identical to, Frank Michelman's view of the *Nollan* case. See Michelman, "Takings, 1987," *Columbia L. Rev.* 88 (1988): 1600, 1608–14.

loss, interfering with legitimate investment-backed expectations. Conversely, if the governmental entity took a traditional property interest outright, either to keep it or to give it to others, the government would have to compensate the owners. Thus, in *Nollan,* for example, the Court assumes, predictably given current practice, that seizing an easement for public beach access would be reviewed as a per se taking.[21] Thus, had the California Coastal Commission simply demanded that the Nollans permit lateral access to their beach, it could have done so only by purchasing an easement through the exercise of eminent domain. The question posed by exaction cases is what to do if the owner voluntarily gives that property interest to the government but does so to receive the government's agreement not to ban development outright. If the Nollans must permit lateral access to be allowed to build along the coast, or if Dolan must dedicate a portion of her property to build a bike path and to act as a greenbelt to help avert creek flooding to be allowed to expand her hardware store and pave over the parking lot, has the state taken lateral access, or a bike path, or a nondevelopment servitude? *Nollan* and *Dolan* suggest that the exaction will be reviewed under the more lenient standards applied to development bans (a form of regulation) if and only if the condition meets the same regulatory end that the ban on building would have met. If the state has not solved the problem that development causes by seizing the easement, it has not really engaged in (deferentially reviewed) regulation at all but rather has used the occasion of the owner's seeking a development permit to seize an easement that the state obviously wanted in any case. Seizing the easement will be reviewed (deferentially) as regulation if and only if doing so is simply a more efficient means of achieving the end that would have been met through deferentially reviewed regulation. In the exaction cases that the Court has decided to date, the property seizure arguably substitutes for a ban on development; conceptually, though, it appears that the relevant question is whether the seizure substitutes for some other deferentially reviewed regulation.[22]

---

21. I question this assumption in the text accompanying chap. 2, n. 46 infra.

22. The reason the ADA and shopping-center-access cases would not be classified as exaction cases, given this narrow reading, is that the state has not, in the Court's view, seized a traditional property interest in either situation. Thus, it is not necessary even to get to the question of whether the state was entitled to do so without being subject to strict review because doing so met the same regulatory end that could have been met through banning or otherwise regulating development. Exaction cases, in this view, involve only cases in which the state clearly seizes property and then attempts to defend the uncompensated seizure as a substitute for noncompensable regulation.

## Governmental Seizures of Traditional Property Rights

In the garden-variety condemnation case, the governmental entity simply purchases a fee interest in the owner's property, transferring title from the original owner to itself. The owner may challenge, generally without success, the entity's right to condemn the property on the grounds that the entity does not plan to make a public use of the seized property[23] or, more often, the owner might challenge the adequacy of the proffered compensation,[24] but the government is unlikely to contest the requirement that it pay some compensation, what it views as the fair market value of the property seized. The government would presumably simply purchase property in a voluntary transaction, without resorting to eminent domain, but for the problems of overcoming holdout problems, particularly in situations in which the state must assemble multiple parcels for large-scale public projects.[25]

---

23. The Supreme Court is extremely deferential to governmental entities' judgment that they have exercised the eminent domain power for a public use, essentially holding that as long as the legislature has some rational public purpose in mind in acquiring and transferring property, the condemnation will be permitted. See, e.g., *Hawaii Housing Authority v. Midkiff,* 467 U.S. 229 (1984) (Hawaii's scheme to redistribute land from a concentrated ownership class to a broader constituency does not constitute an illicit taking for the benefit of the private parties who receive the land); *Berman v. Parker,* 348 U.S. 26 (1964) (the fact that the District of Columbia Redevelopment Act used eminent domain power to purchase slum property for lease or sale to private parties did not mean that the seizure lacked public purpose). Some state courts have been less deferential under parallel state constitutional provisions. See, e.g., *In re City of Seattle,* 96 Wn. 2d 616, 638 P. 2d 549 (1981) (city could not condemn property to be transferred to commercial retailers even though a stated purpose of the condemnation was to forestall inner-city decay and the condemned land was to be developed according to a city-approved plan containing public infrastructure, including a park and an art museum); *Estate of Waggoner v. Gelhorn,* 378 S.W. 2d 47 (Tex. 1964) (statute permitting landlocked owner ingress and egress easement over land of neighbor is unconstitutional not only because neighbor received no compensation but because "it purports to authorize the taking of private property for a private purpose").

24. For a discussion of issues involving the adequacy of compensation, see Julius L. Sackman, *Nichols on Eminent Domain,* 3d ed. (Albany: Bender, 1996), vol. 3, §8.06.

25. See Richard Posner, *Economic Analysis of Law,* 4th ed. (Boston: Little Brown, 1992), 56–57. Sellers of even single parcels might hold out as well if they owned land that the state has somehow precommitted to purchasing. It is difficult to say whether governmental entities bear higher costs than do private parties in altering plans to which governments become institutionally/bureaucratically committed and thus are vulnerable to sellers seeking to capture the buyer's site-specific surplus inherent in having precommitted to a particular site. Compare, e.g., Thomas Merrill, "The Economics of Public Use," *Cornell L. Rev.* 72 (1986): 61, 81–82 (assembly through private voluntary transactions, using buying agents, option agreements, and straw transactions, would typically be less plausible for governments because they usually seek to acquire larger, more site-dependent parcels than do private developers and because governments would find it difficult to maintain secrecy and control opportunities for corruption), with Patricia Munch, "An Economic Analysis of Eminent Domain," *J. of Pol.*

Takings-law controversies all concern transactions that do not so clearly fall into the "forced purchase of a fee" model. At times, the state or local government may enact what it views as a regulation of use, disposition, or exclusion rights, asserting that because it has left title in the hands of the owner, the government has not taken title but has simply changed (or regulated) the terms on which what remains the owner's property may be enjoyed. Owners, however, will assert that the regulation amounts to the seizure of a traditional property interest, for which they are entitled to compensation.

The Court appears to evaluate the owners' position based on what I would describe as narrow, law-school-graduates' conventionalism. (The characterization is thus not based, in my view, on widely shared or even understood social conventions or on a conceptual, logical, or policy-based argument. The fact that the Court's position is not, in my mind, socially conventional but intraprofessionally conventional makes me skeptical of Ackerman's view that title seizure cases reflect an "ordinary observer's" view of what property is, but I have rather little faith and no intellectual or moral investment in this skepticism.)[26] If the state has seized[27] the sort of entitlement that law students study and name in first year property classes, the state will owe compensation.[28] If, though, the state uses (or allows oth-

---

*Econ.* 84 (1976): 473 (eminent domain has not been demonstrated to be the most effective means of coping with parcel-assemblage issues).

26. See Ackerman, *Private Property.* To the degree that Michelman believes the title seizure cases make sense because citizens generally are more prone to be demoralized when simple ownership is compromised, I am obviously equally skeptical that the case law is comprehensible since the cases protect interests that are by no means the most conventional thing-ownership, exclusion-style interests.

27. Seizure occurs when the owner is forced to transfer title to the state. It can also occur if the state permanently occupies the property for its own use or terminates the owner's title. The government is also deemed to seize property if it transfers title or a license to occupancy for the permanent use of some designated third party or parties.

28. The borderline cases involve private land-use-planning devices: easements appear to the Court relatively, though incompletely, property-like. That easements represent the borderline case was clear in Justice Marshall's discussion in *Loretto,* where he writes: "Although the easement of passage, not being a permanent occupation of land, was not considered a taking *per se, Kaiser Aetna* reemphasizes that a physical invasion is a government intrusion of an unusually serious character" (*Loretto v. Teleprompter Manhattan CATV Corp.,* 458 U.S. 419, 437 [1982]). Historically, the benefits of covenants and equitable servitudes appeared to courts to be merely valued entitlements deriving from contract rather than titlelike property interests and owners did not receive compensation when their value was impaired or destroyed by government action. See e.g., *Freisen v. Glendale,* 209 Cal. 524, 288 P. 1080 (1930), *Moses v. Hazen,* 69 F. 2d 842 (App. D.C. 1934). The trend in modern cases, however, is to compensate when the state conduct destroys the benefit of a covenant or servitude. See, e.g., *Southern California Edison Company v. Bourgerie,* 9 Cal. 3d 169, 107 Cal. Rptr. 76, 507 P. 2d 964 (1973); *Horst v. Housing Authority,* 166 N.W. 2d 119 (Neb. 1969). For a good summary of the changes in the case law, see Sackman, *Nichols on Eminent Domain,* vol. 2, §5.07(4).

ers to use or terminates) some other entitlement, no matter how valuable, that is not traditionally deemed a property right, in a conventional property course, rather than a traditional or contract-based interest,[29] the state will simply be deemed to regulate. (Thus, owners may well be as interested in the right to sell property at market prices as they are in the right to devise it or to exclude some undesired class of patrons while allowing others in, but the Court does not find that owners stripped of the traditional entitlement to charge willing buyers what they will pay or traditional exclusion rights have a tenable takings claim.)[30]

I believe that recognizing intraprofessional conventional ideas of core property interests should help predict the distinctions drawn in current takings jurisprudence. Nonetheless, the idea that this or any other account of the cases is complete would be misleading: the results of the cases are surely radically underdetermined given any theory. It would surely be eminently reasonable for a legal conventionalist to describe each of the cases in which the Court found that a traditional, conventional property interest had been seized as enacting mere regulations and, conversely, to describe a substantial number of regulations that are immunized from per se takings treatment as seizures of traditional, legally conventional property rights.

Take, for example, *Loretto v. Teleprompter Manhattan CATV Corp.*,[31] which concerned a New York City ordinance requiring that apartment owners allow installation of cable television cables and boxes on their buildings to benefit tenants desiring cable access. In his majority

---

29. Thus, in *Andrus v. Allard,* 444 U.S. 51 (1979), the Court upholds provisions of the Eagle Protection Act and the Migratory Bird Treaty Act that precluded the sale of eagle feathers, including those acquired before the act. Obviously, the ordinary entitlement to be able to sell property is highly valued, but the right to sell is not studied in conventional property courses in the same way as the devise and bequest of traditional interests (which were limited by the statute invalidated in *Hodel v. Irving*). Of course, Justice Scalia, joined by Chief Justice Rehnquist and Justice Powell, believed the distinction between the lost entitlements in *Hodel* and *Andrus* was unduly slender to sustain and therefore argued that *Andrus* should be limited to its facts (*Hodel v. Irving,* 481 U.S., 704, 719 (1986), but the more law-school-conventionalist view held sway.

30. See, e.g., *FCC v. Florida Power Corp.* 480 U.S. 245 (1987) (upholding price limits on utility companies' charges for cable TV operators); *Block v. Hirsh,* 256 U.S. 135 (1921) (upholding a rent-control statute) . Similarly, neither owners who wish to discriminate against African American patrons nor those who want to exclude political speakers from a commercial shopping center have been able to make a tenable takings claim, since it appears awkward, conventionally, to describe the state in these cases as having seized an easement for use of the property by undesired patrons rather than having limited the ways in which the owner could exercise the access license already granted to the undifferentiated mass of public licensees. In physicalist property terms, the regulation did not mandate any increase or significant change in the physical use of the land. See *Heart of Atlanta Motel Inc. v. United States,* 379 U.S. 241, 261 (1964); *Prune Yard Shopping Center v. Robins,* 447 U.S. 74 (1980).

31. 458 U.S. 419 (1982).

opinion, Justice Marshall found that the ordinance seized the owner's property, entirely on the ground that what the Court presumed to be permanent physical occupancy of a portion of the landlord's building by the authorized third-party cable company amounted to the loss of a fee interest in a very small space via transfer to the cable company.[32]

The Court distinguished the regulations at issue in the case, rather unpersuasively, from a seemingly parallel set of regulations that required landlords to provide certain physical goods on their premises (e.g., mailboxes, fire extinguishers, smoke detectors) on the ostensible ground that the owners required to provide mailboxes and the like maintain title to the property containing the mailbox or smoke detector.[33] But it is hardly clear that an owner's property is fully physically occupied by the relevant third party (cable company) in this case since the company does not gain title to the portions of the building on which the objects sit and would have to remove the cable boxes if, say, the landlord no longer served residential tenants in the building. Conversely, it is not clear that the owner's property is not occupied when a third party's wishes and agenda absolutely dictate how landlords can use their nominal space, and landlords cannot remove their mailboxes, smoke alarms, or fire extinguishers from the space regardless of the landlords' desires. The distinction between the regulations that are permitted without compensation and those that require payment, then, is hardly an obvious one to those attempting to track conventional understandings of property rights in making constitutional judgments.[34]

Not only does the mandate that was invalidated in *Loretto* closely resemble regulations requiring that landlords provide certain services and physical amenities to their tenants, but it could also readily be interpreted as a price-control statute, which the Court has invariably upheld against Takings Clause challenges.[35] One would expect that in a fully competitive

---

32. Ibid., 435 n.12 ("Property rights in a physical thing have been described as the rights to possess, use and dispose of it. . . . To the extent that the government permanently occupied physical property, it effectively destroys *each* of these rights.").

33. Ibid., 440 (Such regulations "do not require the landlord to suffer the physical occupation of a portion of his building by a third party.").

34. To track the Court's language in *Loretto* condemning only the regulatory program mandating cable access rather than those mandating mail or utilities access, one would note that the landlord has lost all of the same possession, use, and disposition rights to the space he must devote to utility hookups or mailboxes as he has as to the cable connection.

35. See, e.g., *Block v. Hirsh* (upholding a regulation that forbids landlords from evicting tenants, even when their leases terminate, so long as the tenants are willing to pay the submarket prices set by a rent-control commission); *FCC v. Florida Power Corp.* (upholding against a takings challenge a decision by the federal government that substantially reduced the rent a utility charged to a cable TV operator).

market, the price that tenants would have to pay to induce their landlords to permit them to hook up to cable would approximate zero, since competitive prices should drop to the cost of provision of a service. The landlords bear no costs from permitting unobtrusive cable hookups, particularly since the statute required that the cable company compensate the landlord if installation caused any real physical damage to the building.[36] The fact that the landlords were able, in an unregulated market, to charge a positive price for the service clearly reflects market failure that is inevitably inherent in the market for housing services, regardless of how many providers of such services are available. All particular landlords have a certain level of quasi-monopoly power over current tenants, given that moving is costly (both directly, with the cost of moving vans, shopping for a new unit, and so forth, and indirectly, as in breaking neighborhood ties, personal attachment to a unit, and so on). Landlords may use high, non-cost-related charges for services that tenants value highly (like cable hookup) as a technique to capture some of the tenant's site-specific surplus, particularly if there are either legal restrictions on raising rents directly or market-based restrictions (explicit or implicit contracts restricting renewal rent increases).

It is possible, too, that the tenants bore none of the costs of the cable hookup, that the cable company already charged a profit-maximizing monopoly price and the landlord simply negotiated with the company to capture some of the company's monopoly rents. Landlord charges to the company, though, might still be regulated for four reasons. First, they might interfere with the city's capacity to regulate cable charges. Second, while the prospect of earning economic rents in the media-access industry may provide desirable incentives to media-access developers, dissipation of these rents by those who hold the land over which the delivery mechanisms must travel serves no obvious social purpose. Third, if the building owners and cable companies fail to agree on how to divide the monopoly surplus, tenants will be deprived of a service for which they would willingly pay. It may be prudent to avoid giving property rights that are of value only to permit an owner to hold up another party for fear that strategic behavior will frustrate efficient transfers.[37] Finally, the cable companies,

---

36. In fact, it is likely that the installation of the cable hookups increased the value of the property as a residential building.

37. Think about the parallel case in which airlines have been granted what could be seen as regulation-grounded passage easements to fly over (and invade the traditional airspace above) parcels. If the ground-dwelling parcel owners maintained the right to exclude the planes, though overflight caused no actual damage, one would expect some to try to hold up

even if unregulated, might well charge a uniform fee that would preclude them from charging all tenants their full reservation prices, as landlords might: obviously, there are some efficiency advantages to increasing price discrimination, but to the degree that the city distributively favors the buyers here, barriers to price discrimination are desirable.

There are several other recent cases in which the Court has assumed, rather hastily, that a per se taking has occurred on the assumption that title has been seized. In each case, though, what is labeled a title seizure could readily be recharacterized. One is *Hodel v. Irving*,[38] in which the Court held that Congress must compensate owners of fractionated beneficial interests in land held by the federal government in trust for Native Americans when the government abrogates the traditional rights either to devise these beneficial tenancies in common or have them pass by descent. But the Court never even considers that the federal government could well have accomplished the same end—stopping all owners of fractionated beneficial shares from passing these interests along at death—simply by charging user fees equal to the costs of administering the distribution of income to fractionated beneficial owners.[39] The failure to see that Congress might have dealt with the problem of fractionation by refusing to continue to subsidize owners who rely on the federal government to provide free accounting services, with precisely the same impact on the effective right to retain, let alone transfer at death, fractionated beneficial interests, misses the conceptual point that the *Nollan* Court aptly recognized in the limited context of development exactions. The government can substitute a traditional taking for a regulatory option (and in this regard, charging user fees might be thought of as akin to regulation) without triggering per se taking treatment as long as doing so is simply a more effective way of meeting the same, permissible regulatory end.

At the same time, the Court frequently characterizes government conduct as merely regulatory when owners might well argue with great force that they have been deprived of a core traditional property right. The

---

the airlines once they had precommitted themselves to a particular flight path. Though the airline company would willingly pay more for overflight rights than the parcel owner's reservation price, some deals might not be struck because of strategic behavior.

38. 481 U.S. 704 (1987).

39. The Court refers to one of the fractionated tracts in its opinion. The annual income from the tract is eight thousand dollars; the largest interest holder receives $82.85 annually. Two-thirds of the owners receive less than one dollar of income a year. Yet the administrative costs of handling the tract are estimated at $17,560 annually, roughly forty dollars per owner (*Hodel,* 712–13).

Court's characterization of the property right the owners were asked to dedicate in *Nollan*—the statement that a physical taking occurs whenever unnamed individuals receive a permanent and continuous right to pass to and fro over the owner's property—seems to apply reasonably well[40] to what the Court deems a regulation rather than a per se taking in *Prune-Yard*. The fact that particular political speakers will leave the shopping center at some point would seem to be of little moment (particular ocean gazers leave the Nollan's backyard too) since speakers, as a group, retain a permanent right to pass to and fro over the center's property and stay in particular places at the center, against the owner's wishes, as long as the center remains in operation.

Similarly, it strikes me that there are at least four plausible interpretations of the statute that the Court validated in *Keystone Bituminous Coal Association v. DeBenedictis,*[41] which sought to prevent subsidence of adjacent property by forbidding coal companies from mining more than half the coal found beneath the ground they owned. The regulation might have been deemed a seizure of two distinct traditional estates held by the companies: first, the neighbors' right of lateral support, which the coal mining companies had previously purchased from adjacent surface owners, an estate that the companies in effect saw transferred back to the initial sellers by the statute; and, second, the subsurface mineral rights to that physical portion of the subsurface area that could not be mined given the regulation. The second possible interpretation is to characterize the action as the seizure of that portion of the coal that could not be mined. Third, it could also be characterized, as a bare majority of the Court did, as a regulation forbidding the noxious misuse of subsurface rights with no cognizable effect on Pennsylvania's support estate, which was invariably incident to either the surface holder's fee or the subsurface mineral rights' holder's. Fourth and finally, it might have been characterized differently than the Court or the parties did. It might have been viewed as a general technique to undo what the legislature characterized as (by and large) unconscionable contracts between subsurface miners and surface owners; rather than resolve, at great cost, questions about whether surface owners were adequately informed about the risks of subsidence or were compensated

---

40. The facts of the cases are, of course, distinguishable. First, there is a higher level of privacy intrusion in *Nollan* than in *PruneYard.* Arguably, the regulation in *PruneYard* affects only what invitees may do on property to which they already have access, while the *Nollan* regulation opens up the property to those who might otherwise be excluded.

41. 480 U.S. 470 (1987).

adequately for waiving support rights, the legislature simply undid contracts that it presumed were (nearly) invariably exploitative.[42]

It is reasonably predictable, though, how many cases, including our ADA case, would be dealt with under this first test. Imagine grocery store owners arguing that they should receive compensation when forced, by Title III of the ADA, to widen the aisles of their establishments to permit wheelchairs to pass. Even if the concomitant loss of shelf space decreases the value of the property, the fact that the wheelchair users will use but not have full-blown title to the widened aisles will almost surely induce the Court to treat this case, in terms of the physical invasion/title seizure line of cases, as more like the mandatory mailbox than the cable hookup.[43] The ADA's demands that a store be physically altered will almost surely be deemed a building regulation, not a transfer of property to a third party.[44]

---

42. Some might argue that if the state were to adopt this last view, the state would concede that it had violated not the Takings Clause but the constitutional prohibition on impairing contracts. See, e.g., Douglas Kmiec, "The Original Understanding of the Takings Clause Is Neither Weak nor Obtuse," *Columbia L. Rev.* 88 (1988): 1630, 1645–46. The view that the contract was unconscionable, though, can readily be understood as a declaration that it was void ab initio and gave rise to no vested contractual rights.

Similarly, the property owners in *Penn Central Transportation Co. v. New York City,* 438 U.S. 104 (1978) lost use and disposition rights in the airspace over Grand Central Terminal, which was just as much a physical part of their parcel as the portions of the building the Court thought were seized in *Loretto.* Conventional property norms hardly dictate the idea that the fee is invaded in *Loretto* because a third party authorized by the state physically occupies the fee but that the fee is not invaded in *Penn Central,* where the state itself takes over a portion of the fee and forbids that any use be made. This characterization would hold not just for *Penn Central* but for garden-variety zoning cases in which, for example, a municipality restricts the height of a building.

Similarly, *Miller v. Schoene,* 276 U.S. 272 (1928), is typically characterized as an early regulatory takings case that upholds the state entomologist's decision under the Cedar Rust Act that owners of certain ornamental red cedar trees had to cut down the trees to prevent the spread of rust disease to nearby apple orchards. The decision would still be upheld, I believe, if it were decided that the owner's relevant property was the land, not the cedar trees, because the decline in value of the land was probably not unduly substantial, especially given the corresponding regulatory gain; however, the title in the trees was certainly destroyed by an order to cut them down as much as landholders' titles in their land were destroyed by floods in the cases Marshall cites as authority in *Loretto* for the proposition that the state cannot seize title in property by destroying it. See Loretto, 427–28 citing, for example, *Pumpelly v. Green Bay Co.,* 13 Wall 166 (1872) *Sanguinetti v. United States,* 264 U.S. 146 (1924).

43. For a district court case making precisely this finding, see *Zahedi v. Pinnock,* 844 F. Supp. 574, 586–87 (S.D. Cal.1993).

44. It is also even clearer that public accommodation owners' desire to exclude the disabled as a result of either their own aversive prejudice or of their belief that other customers might be averse to people with disabilities will not raise a takings issue, even though it limits historic fuller-blown rights to exclude. See *Heart of Atlanta Motel.* While an owner may be permitted to exclude the public entirely, his interest in picking and choosing which members of the public to serve has not been treated as a basic incident of property.

Though I am fairly confident in this conclusion, it is hardly unexceptionable. Obviously, the aisle dedication can be distinguished from the transfer in *Loretto* itself, in which the third party (cable company) received full title to a very small portion of the owner's land, at least as long as the owner operated the building as an apartment block. But the harder claim for ADA proponents to counter would be that Title III demands the granting of an easement much like the bike path easement demanded in *Dolan,* an easement that the Court simply assumes constitutes a *Loretto*-style compensable taking.[45] Thus, regulated public accommodation owners will claim that just like Dolan, they retain general fee ownership of their property but must leave a portion of it undeveloped so that third parties (bikers in *Dolan,* the physically disabled in this case) can cross it.

Public accommodation owners will further argue that the most straightforward, ready-at-hand arguments on behalf of Title III—that it is no different than any structural regulation in a building code (e.g., a requirement to leave space open near fire exits) or use regulation (e.g., the *PruneYard* requirement to allow orderly picketing by invitees or the *Heart of Atlanta* requirement that public accommodation owners not discriminate among invitees on the basis of race)—are inadequate. Pickets or African American patrons with whom the racist owner would otherwise refuse to deal add no physical intrusion nor do they require any change in the building's physical structure. And traditional building codes (e.g., those requiring space around fire exits) may be necessary to protect against traditional harm causing: in this sense, despite the ostensible separation of *Loretto* from the rest of the takings cases, it may be impossible to assess *Loretto* claims without some inquiry into distinct, nonphysicalist issues like whether the disputed regulation confers general benefits or precludes harms.

Still, I am quite sure of my prediction that owners would be granted no compensation for the costs of complying with Title III if the Supreme Court were to review the statute. The Dolans are not allowed to exclude bike riders generally; they are not just unable to exclude bike use by people who would be on their land anyway. On the other hand, the easement purportedly granted by Title III is enjoyed only by invitees, who gain no

45. Such a per se taking may nonetheless be noncompensable if it simply substitutes for an alternative permissible regulation. I addressed and will address in more detail how current takings jurisprudence would deal with such an exaction.

title or access rights beyond that of any other invitee.[46] Moreover, I strongly suspect a public accommodation owner's *Loretto* claim will fail in part because if it succeeded, the Court's jurisprudence in this area would unravel even further than it has already: the requirement that the owner make certain architectural modifications (e.g., building ramps) would be immune from review (since no obvious property right like an easement is granted to third parties), while a precisely functionally parallel requirement, typically part of the same judicial or administrative order, that barriers be removed to empty out space for mobility-impaired customers to navigate might lead to a claim for compensation.

**Government Destroys Virtually All Property Value**

Assume now that the government clearly leaves formal title in the hands of the owner. Moreover, the government does not permanently physically occupy or authorize the occupation of the property or destroy it. The government will still presumptively be deemed to have taken the property if the property is subject to regulations that deny an owner "all economically beneficial or productive viable use of [his] land."[47] The state may rebut the presumption that it owes the owner compensation only by showing that the regulation takes nothing the owner really owned because it simply precludes conduct that would not be allowed in any case, given the state's law of property and nuisance.[48]

---

46. Moreover, I suspect (though I think it is by no means settled law) that if all people in Tigard, not just the Dolans, whose land abutted the Fasano Creek had to dedicate some land to a bike path (or if all coastal owners in California had to allow access from the road in the *Nollan* context), one would not say that the state had seized an easement. What animates Dolan's claim is that some creek-fronting owners are singled out to dedicate some portion of their land to a third party, while others are exempt from that requirement. The fact that all store owners must insure accessibility rather than some particular owner or small subset of owners being asked to redesign badly hurts the hypothetical owner's *Loretto/Dolan* claim.

47. *Lucas v. South Carolina Coastal Council,* 505 U.S. 1003 (1992). See also *Agins v. Tiburon,* 447 U.S. 255, 260 (1980).

48. Thus, in *Lucas,* Justice Scalia states that new legislation or declarations that prohibit all economically beneficial use of land are invalid (in the absence of compensation) unless the limitations "inhere in the title itself, in the restrictions that background principles of the State's law of property and nuisance already place upon land ownership. A law or decree with such an effect, in other words, do no more than duplicate the result that could have been achieved in the courts—by adjacent landowners . . . under the State's law of private nuisance, or by the State under its complementary power to abate nuisances that affect the public generally" (505 U.S. 1029).

The test is ambiguous in application, both because of the problems of severance (could the owner subdivide property interests, whether spatially or conceptually, in such a fashion that there is no economically viable use of the subdivided property?)[49] and because of the problems of determining whether the sorts of regulations most likely to be reviewed in these contexts, environmental protection–based bans on development, proscribe behavior that an emerging law of nuisance might proscribe.[50] The test may be unappealing as well: whether a modern legislature's determination that certain behavior is unacceptable ought to be weighed less highly than the judgment of the nineteenth-century judges who framed traditional nuisance-abatement law is questionable.[51]

---

49. This is the dominant theme in Justice Stevens's dissent in *Lucas*. ("[D]evelopers and investors may market specialized estates to take advantage of the Court's new rule. The smaller the estate, the more likely that regulatory change will effect a total taking. Thus, an investor may, for example, purchase the right to build a multifamily home on a specific lot, with the result that a zoning regulation that allows only single-family homes would render the investor's property interest 'valueless'" [ibid., 1065–66].) The concept of conceptual severance derives from Margaret Jane Radin, "The Liberal Conception of Property: Cross-Currents in the Jurisprudence of Takings," *Columbia L. Rev.* 88 (1988): 1667, 1676.

In his opinion for the Court, *id.*, 1045, n. 7, Justice Scalia argues that the court should forbid some forms of conceptual severance (the division of property into novel use rights not historically recognized). He does not directly address either the issue of physical severance, which is not germane to the *Lucas* case itself, or issues of severance into property rights that were historically recognized (e.g., subsurface mineral extraction rights or support rights), which might be rendered substantially valueless, though the underlying fee was not, by the regulations that were subject to balancing tests in both *Pennsylvania Coal v. Mahon* (260 U.S. 393 [1922]) and *Keystone Bituminous Coal Association. v. DeBenedictis* (480 U.S. 470 [1987]). The Court in *Keystone* upheld a Pennsylvania regulation that required coal-mining companies to leave 50 percent of the coal beneath the land supporting certain buildings in place, notwithstanding the facts that the company could not use a large physical portion of the subsurface and that all purchased support rights were rendered valueless since the company was now required by statute to do what it would have had to do but for the purchase of the support rights.

50. Justice Scalia solves this second problem pretty much by fiat, declaring that certain "extensions" of nuisance law to novel settings do not represent "objectively reasonable application of relevant precedents" (*Lucas v. South Carolina Coastal Council*, 1032, n. 18). I think he is right to say that one can predict what Justice Scalia would call a reasonable application of nuisance law, and if the decision is read to hold that the state can avoid the obligation to pay compensation only if it is abating what a conservative judge with a strong libertarian bent is likely to think is a nuisance, it is probably coherent. But state courts have extended nuisance law in fashions that would doubtless have seemed objectively unreasonable to Justice Scalia. For example, holdings that builders might create a nuisance when they block access to light needed to operate solar-powered batteries, as in *Prah v. Maretti*, 321 N.W. 2d 182 (Wis. 1987), would not seem to all readers to be applications of precedent.

51. This is probably the main concern animating Justice Blackmun's dissent in *Lucas*. ("Even more perplexing . . . is the Court's reliance on common-law principles of nuisance in its quest for a value-free takings jurisprudence. In determining what is a nuisance at common

There is no doubt in my mind, though, that the test will not apply to the vast bulk of the regulatory taxation I will examine in this book: whether the test applies to any regulations other than hyperrestrictive use plans designed to protect fragile ecosystems is dubious.[52] Clearly, for example, public accommodation owners whose profits might be lower because of the requirement to comply with the ADA by installing costly ramps or widening aisles in a fashion that reduces space for inventory will not be able to claim that there is no economically viable use of their property once the regulatory scheme is enforced or to argue that an inquiry should be conducted about whether the portion of her property now devoted to access is valueless.[53]

## Standard Regulations

If the Court decides that the regulation does not seize title in the sense I have described or destroy all economically viable uses, the regulation will be evaluated under the balancing test best articulated in *Penn Central*

---

law, state courts make exactly the decision that the Court finds so troubling when made by the South Carolina General Assembly today; they determine whether the use is harmful. Common-law public and private nuisance law is simply a determination whether a particular use causes harm. . . . There is nothing magical in the reasoning of judges long dead" [*Lucas v. South Carolina Coastal Council,* 1054–55] [citations omitted]). To the degree that Justice Scalia was arguing, at least implicitly, that current owners were themselves to blame if and only if they paid the price the property would command if it could be developed in a situation in which prior judicial holdings made the belief it could be developed unreasonable, he is moving away from the per se rule he announces to a balancing test demanding that owners show they have been deprived of legitimate investment-backed expectations.

52. Even then, the test applies only on the assumption that the more passive forms of ownership are not reasonably valuable. Justice Kennedy, concurring in *Lucas,* expressed substantial skepticism about the finding by the South Carolina Court of Common Pleas that the regulated property had no significant market value or resale potential (*Lucas v. South Carolina Coastal Council,* 1033–34), and Justice Blackmun, in dissent, emphasizes that the parcel certainly has consumption value, which he believed rendered the lower court's finding "clearly erroneous" (505 U.S., 1044: "Petitioner can picnic, swim, camp in a tent, or live on the property in a movable trailer. State courts frequently have recognized that land has economic value where the only residual economic uses are recreation or camping.")

53. See *Zahedi v. Pinnock,* 587–88. It is a quirky academic question, of no practical moment, whether owners would succeed even if the Court allowed them to sever their property (physically rather than conceptually) and analyze whether the empty aisle space was truly rendered valueless by the regulation in question. While it is lucid that owners would generate more revenue if they could use the space for inventory rather than for wider aisles— otherwise, they would make the change spontaneously, without the regulation—wider aisles may well draw both disabled and nondisabled customers to the store, thus generating some value. The regulation is not akin to a hypothetical regulation in which the state demanded that a portion of the store had to be simply walled off, of no use to anyone.

*Transportation Co. v. City of New York.*[54] While the Court will not declare such regulations to be per se compensable takings, it might nonetheless demand the governmental entity compensate owners taking due account of (a) the economic impact of the regulation (the degree to which the net value of the owner's properly aggregated property value diminishes, accounting not only for the losses the owner suffers as a result of the limitations on use rights but the gains the owner enjoys because similarly situated property is subject to the same regulations); (b) the character of the government action (particularly whether it meets some significant public end to alter the conduct of the particular owner); and (c) whether the action interferes with reasonable investment-backed expectations (that is, whether the owner will bear an out-of-pocket loss as a result of paying a price for the property that reflected a reasonable expectation of being able to develop it in the now-proscribed fashion).[55]

There is not a great deal to say about how a particularistic balancing test will work in practice. The Court has never articulated quantitatively what constitutes the sort of substantial decline in property value[56] that

---

54. 438 U.S. 104 (1978) (upholding a historic-preservation ordinance that precluded owners of Grand Central Station and other "historic monuments" from altering the external structure of the building without approval, as applied to a city agency decision to prohibit the owner from building a skyscraper in the airspace over the station).

55. The Court has never adequately explained why it is so much more solicitous of those who bear out-of-pocket rather than opportunity-cost losses. (The solicitousness extended, quite early on, to zoning cases where there was thought to be substantial constitutional protection for nonconforming uses but almost none for owners who planned but had not yet made uses banned by the zoning plan.) It seems reasonably clear why one would be more solicitous of those out-of-pocket losses not caused by owners' negligent beliefs that they would forever be free from the challenged regulation than of those losses grounded in such negligence. There would, in the absence of such a rule, be a serious moral-hazard problem: just as it is undesirable to have a party construct an expensive home on an empty parcel just before the state condemns the fee, and just as it is reasonable to restrict compensation awards under the belief that the home was constructed after the party did or should have known that the condemnation would occur, any rule that compensates people for all they have spent encourages people to spend without regard to the possibility of the relevant casualty (condemnation or regulation). This point is emphasized in Louis Kaplow, "An Economic Analysis of Legal Transitions," *Harvard L. Rev.* 99 (1986): 509, 529–30, 537–42. However, any rule that protects only those who have invested more money than the property is now worth given the regulation, rather than those who experience equally substantial paper losses, seems to distinguish, for reasons that are not especially clear, between recent property buyers and those who have held property for a substantial period.

56. The Court has also not given precise conceptual or practical guidance that would permit judgment of whether owners have gained the sort of special benefits from the existence of the regulatory scheme being challenged that would give pause in measuring the net losses suffered simply by ascertaining the difference between the postregulation value of the property and its value if freed from regulation. Take the *Penn Central* case: if the owner could sell the

would typically trigger careful scrutiny,[57] let alone standards that would help to determine whether particular levels of private losses are nonetheless acceptable because legitimate public purposes are served by regulating this particular party. At some level the Court is trying to figure out when a particular owner is unduly singled out to bear burdens that ought to be more widely spread, but stating this fact does little more than restate a general purpose of the Takings Clause.

Many cases, though, are readily decided once classified as garden-variety regulations cases, in part because it is quite clear that the Supreme Court will rarely, if ever, find that a garden-variety regulation causes a compensable taking.[58] It is clear, for instance, that the ADA, on its face, will be held not to take property, since it demands only reasonable accommodations and a Court would limit public accommodation owners' obligations in such a way that they would never be deemed to lose too much.

---

property for 100 percent more if permitted to build in the airspace over Grand Central Station, did the regulation cause a 50 percent decline in the property's value? What if the property would not be worth 100 percent more than its current value without the existence of historic-preservation regulations that improved real estate values in the immediate vicinity? In New York City more generally? What if the value of the regulated property is substantially enhanced by the presence of land-use planning regulations more generally, though not the historic-preservation program in particular, some of which bears more heavily on other owners than it does on these owners?

57. Courts were inconsistent in deciding when a particular loss of value was excessive. "Ordinances which variously diminished property values from $1,500,000 to $275,000, $450,000 to $50,000, and $65,000 to $5,000 have all been upheld. Ordinances that reduced property values from about $48,750 to about $11,250 and from $350,000 to $100,000 have been struck down" ("Developments in the Law—Zoning," *Harvard L. Rev.* 91 [1978]: 1427, 1480). Generally, owners have been unsuccessful in inverse-condemnation cases even when the property's value declined substantially. See, e.g., *William C. Haas and Co. v. City and County of San Francisco*, 605 F. 2d 1117 (9th Cir. 1979) (upholding rezoning that reduced value of property by roughly 95 percent); *HFH Ltd. v. Superior Court*, 15 Cal. 3d 508, 125 Cal. Rptr. 365, 542 P. 2d 237 *cert. denied* 425 U.S. 904 (1975) (upholding regulation resulting in an 80 percent decline in property value); *Pace Resources, Inc. v. Shrewsbury Township*, 808 F. 2d 1023 (3d Cir. 1987) (upholding regulation that led to 89 percent reduction in property value). There are exceptions, particularly in somewhat older cases. See, e.g., *Sinclair Pipe Line Co. v. Village of Richton Park*, 19 Ill. 2d 370, 167 N.E. 2d 406 (1960) , and *Pearce v. Village of Edina*, 263 Minn. 553, 118 N.W. 2d 659 (1962) (rezoning causing roughly 75 percent decline in value held to be compensable inverse condemnation).

58. There are exceptions. See *Pennsylvania Coal Co. v. Mahon* (first case to hold that a state must compensate for a regulatory taking that went too far as well as for direct appropriations of property, invalidating Pennsylvania's Kohler Act, which forbade the mining of anthracite coal in such a fashion as to cause the subsidence of most human habitations, even where the mining companies had purchased waivers of damage claims by surface owners). But the case might well be deemed to be restricted to its facts given the holding in *Keystone Bituminous Coal.*

It is implausible that the Court could construe the ADA to impose the sorts of large-scale losses on property that trigger effective demands for compensation.[59]

## Exactions

In certain circumstances, developers will be permitted to develop their property if and only if they comply with a particular condition. In exchange for permission to develop, they must supply something the governmental entity wants: an easement, parks, sewage connections, money for the city to construct new infrastructure. Reading these cases narrowly, the Court analyzes exactions in three steps.

First, the Court asks whether the government could take the thing the developer agrees to supply in exchange for the building permit, without paying compensation, assuming that there were no reciprocal promises by the government to grant the owner some privilege to which it has no categorical entitlement. Thus far, Supreme Court exactions cases involve situations in which the governmental entity conditions development on the owner agreeing to surrender title to some portion of his property.[60] Thus, in *Nollan,* for instance, the Court assumes that the California Coastal Commission could not have made the Nollans allow public access to the ocean across their property without condemning the property and paying for the public right of way. (In my view, the assumption is not clearly justified, but it was not called into question by the dissenters in the case. While the state of California almost surely lacks the constitutional authority to demand public access from a *subset* of similarly situated beachfront property owners, a state rule that more generally redefined the incidents of owning oceanfront property, limiting, for example, the capacity to exclude those who cross from the road, much as owners at common law have been unable to exclude many of those seeking lateral access, below the high-tide mark, should have been unproblematic under any nonlibertarian view of the Takings Clause.)[61] Similarly, in *Dolan,* the Court assumes that the city of Tigard would have had to condemn some of the store owner's property

---

59. For conclusions consonant with this view, see *Zahedi v. Pinnock,* 588.

60. One could imagine, hypothetically, a municipality conditioning development on compliance with a regulation that constituted a taking under *Penn Central,* but such cases have not arisen. It is impossible even to imagine what it might mean to condition a development permit on compliance with a regulation that rendered the property economically valueless, under *Lucas,* since no rational developer would accept such an offer.

61. See Michelman, "Takings, 1987," 1610–12, for a parallel argument.

to permit a bike path to be built over it or to dedicate some to a structure-free floodplain to permit improvement of the storm-drainage system along the creek.

Second, the Court asks whether the governmental entity should be permitted to escape its prima facie obligation to pay compensation for the seizure of the property interest. The government may do so if and only if the property seizure is nothing more than a more efficacious substitute for permissible direct regulation of the owner's activity. (It is tempting, but I think ultimately less helpful, to ask whether what is exacted from the developer solves the problem that development creates. It often will not matter which way one formulates the test, but one can imagine plausible hypotheticals in which the distinct formulations matter. For example, imagine a municipality that demanded that a developer of low-income housing provide funds for social services more frequently needed by low-income residents or private security forces to deal with what is presumed to be a higher crime rate associated with poverty, just as developers must often pay infrastructure fees. A court could distinguish the cases factually—arguing that it is more difficult for a municipality to prove either that low-income residents use any class of services or commit crimes more frequently than do other residents or that the presence of a particular low-income housing project in the municipality increases rather than relocates the low-income population than it is to prove that new housing increases the need for sewage or utility lines. But I suspect that it is not necessary to reach the factual issues. Whether it is the case, in fact, that many zoning decisions that effectively squeeze out low-income housing are predicated on desires for social segregation and service-cost avoidance, such are not permissible municipal goals. Since one could not ban low-income development to avoid social problems associated with the poor, one cannot condition a building permit to house them on solving those social problems.)

Direct regulation is almost always permissible under the *Penn Central* test. Thus, if the governmental entity can demonstrate that the seizure of title is nothing more than an alternative mechanism for meeting a goal that might otherwise have been achieved through direct regulation, it is overwhelmingly likely that the seizure will be sustained. Thus, in *Nollan,* the Court asks first, in this regard, whether the Coastal Commission could have forbidden the owners from building altogether.[62] Assuming, as the

---

62. "Given, then, that requiring uncompensated conveyance of the easement outright would violate the Fourteenth Amendment . . . [w]e assume, without deciding, that . . . the Commission unquestionably would be able to deny the Nollans their permit outright"

Court does, that the answer to that question is the predictable yes, the Court next asks whether the governmental entity accomplishes the end it would have met through the development ban by seizing the title the owner surrendered. Had the Coastal Commission decided to ban development to protect the public's visual access to the beach, the commission could have, without compensation, instead demanded that the developer provide a viewing place (on or off the property) as a condition of development, since to do so would simply be an alternative means to meet a permissible regulatory end. But because the Coastal Commission demanded physical access, it did not attempt to meet the same regulatory end but simply to extort an easement from a party dependent on the state for a building permit.[63] (As the dissenters and a number of commentators have noted, the *Nollan* majority takes a rather narrow view of the required

---

(*Nollan v. California Coastal Commission*, 834–35). The Court's decision in this regard is premised both on the supposition that the Coastal Commission would have a reasonable purpose in forbidding the building—that the commission's claim that it was reasonable to protect the public's ability to see the beach to overcome "psychological barriers" to using the beach—and on the supposition that such a development ban would not interfere drastically with the Nollans' use of the property. That is simply to say that the decision would be reviewed under the deferential standard of *Penn Central.* The reason the denial of the building permit would not have given rise to a *Lucas* claim—that a per se taking had occurred unless the regulation abated a common law nuisance because it left the owner without any viable use of his property—is that the owners of the Nollans' property (the Nollans' landlords) could themselves have repaired the bungalow on the property without applying for a permit to construct a brand-new structure.

63. "[T]he condition would be constitutional even if it consisted of the requirement that the Nollans provide a viewing spot on their property for passersby with whose sighting of the ocean their new house would interfere. Although such a requirement, constituting a permanent grant of continuous access to the property, would have to be considered a taking if not attached to a development permit, the Commission's assumed power to forbid construction of the house in order to protect the public's view of the beach must surely include the power to condition construction upon some concession by the owner, even a concession of property rights, that serves the same end. . . . It is quite impossible to understand how a requirement that people already on the public beaches be able to walk across the Nollans' property reduces any obstacles to viewing the beach created by the new house" (ibid., 836–38).

Viewed as a case about unconstitutional conditions, it would be helpful, perhaps, to follow up on the analogy the Court itself uses. It would be permissible, presumably, to forbid a person from shouting "Fire!" in a crowded theater. But it would not be permissible to say that the government could condition the right to shout "Fire!" in a theater on payment of a hundred dollars, though doing so is a less restrictive regulation of speech. Forbidding shouting "Fire!" is permissible under the First Amendment, given various balances between public-safety interests and desires to protect expressive speech. Similarly, forbidding development without compensation may be permitted under the Takings Clause of the Fifth Amendment, given the state's police power. But conditioning the exercise of First or Fifth Amendment rights on the payment of money (or property) is unacceptable, largely to insure government evenhandedness and the preservation of a strong private sphere immune from indirect government control. See Kathleen Sullivan, "Unconstitutional Conditions," *Har-*

nexus between the exaction and the regulatory alternative, assuming that the Coastal Commission could have banned to protect only view and thus could exact only property rights that restored view. If, however, the state seeks to retain a certain degree of psychic public access to the ocean or nonexclusivity, increasing the ability to walk across the beach may partly offset the existence of a bigger private home.[64] Of course, if a nexus test is going to make any sense at all, there must be some limits on substitutability: if all psychic end states can be commodified, the losses from development can always be stated in dollar terms, and the developer can always be asked to provide some service or property worth an equivalent amount in dollar terms or the dollars themselves. The Court, though, would be in no position at all to review the locality's claim that development generated a particular dollar level of psychic loss.)

Third, the Court asks whether the exaction more than substitutes for the regulatory alternative, whether the state entity not only meets the regulatory purpose by demanding payment in cash or property but gains something additional.[65] Thus, in *Dolan*, the Court concedes that the

---

*vard L. Rev.* 102 (1989): 1413, 1492–97. One knows that the state is simply conditioning the exercise of such rights on payment of money or property rather than meeting a proper regulatory purpose if the condition does not advance the regulatory purpose. To follow the analogy with a rather odd hypothetical, it might be constitutionally acceptable for a state to condition the right to shout "Fire!" on adding wider aisles and doors or other things that would better insure that no one was hurt during panicky mass escapes, because the condition would be an alternative method of meeting the permitted (First Amendment) regulatory purpose (public safety), just as a view easement (but not an access one) is an alternative way of meeting the permitted (Fifth Amendment) regulatory purpose (insuring public view).

64. *Nollan,* 845–87 (J. Brennan dissenting), 865 (J. Blackmun dissenting). Whether one believes the state is really solving a problem or engaging in a plan of extortion depends in significant part on whether one believes the state is fundamentally benevolent or a roving thief. See Margaret Jane Radin, "Evaluating Government Reasons for Changing Property Regimes," *Albany L. Rev.* 55 (1992): 597, 600–603.

65. The Court assumes, without much argument, that the developer can be asked, constitutionally, to undo the entire incremental impact of its development in exchange for permission to develop, even though there is little reason to believe the developer is, in any discernable sense, the unique source of a problem simply because it is last in time. Assume, for example, that the hardware store expansion the *Dolan* petitioners propose will bring in one hundred new cars each afternoon; the Court is clear that the city can seize a bikeway easement whose effect is to get (somewhere not much in excess of) one hundred additional citizens of Tigard to switch from cars to bikes. (If substantially more people switch, the exaction will fail the rough proportionality test that the required dedication is related in "extent to the impact of the proposed development" [*Dolan v. City of Tigard,* 391].) But the congestion problem is caused just as much by the preexisting store owners as the developer; if the developer has any sort of cognizable fairness claim that citizens generally should pay for an easement that takes more than a hundred cars off the road, the developer would seem to have just as good a fairness claim that other store owners should contribute to easements that cover one hundred car displacements.

seizure of the bike path easement may well meet the same sort of regulatory end that banning the expansion of the owner's downtown hardware store would (avoiding auto traffic congestion) and that seizing land for the floodplain also met the same end as the ban on paving over the parking lot would meet (minimizing flood danger). But the Court worried that the *Nollan* test would become procedurally a mere formal pleading requirement and that municipalities would attempt to seize property without compensation, using as a pretext the possibility that seizing the property simply served a regulatory end.[66] Perhaps, too, the Court worried that even if the governmental entity was not using the seizure as a pretext—that it actually would have chosen to ban the development rather than permit it without some compensating property right—the government should not seize too much of the owner's development surplus but simply end up indifferent between development with the condition and nondevelopment or in a better position if and only if the government could not tailor a less intrusive exaction that simply met more precisely the problem development created.

I believe that *Dolan* was a very badly decided case, even accepting both the legal and persuasive authority of *Nollan*. This is partly true for institutional competence reasons. *Nollan* demands a task that judges can readily accomplish: it asks only whether there is a conceptual nexus between the exaction and the aim of the regulation for which the exaction might arguably substitute. If not, the exaction is a taking. A modest extension of *Nollan* might have been possible: trial courts might be competent to ascertain whether a governmental entity fabricated a regulatory purpose for an exaction pretextually. The courts are simply not competent to ascertain, however, whether the entity wound up in a substantially better position as a result of the exaction than it would have had it simply banned the development and thereby violates *Dolan*'s rough proportionality test. Thus, for example, the Court recognizes that the expanded store will

---

66. Owners have a legitimate fear: *Nollan* says that the state cannot seize an easement without paying by conditioning issuance of any old building permit on the owner's granting the easement. Only if the easement seizure meets the same purpose that denying the permit would have met can the state seriously claim that it did not have an independent plan to seize the easement, unconnected to the development, that should be funded out of general tax funds because it was a general, independent public project. But what if the state really wants the easement (for the greenway or the bike path in *Dolan,* for lateral access in *Nollan*) for completely independent reasons but is able to show a tenuous relationship between the conditions and the problems that building would have created? If one could not seize the greenway if building did not at all contribute to flooding, why should doing so be possible if it contributed a thimbleful of water to the flooding problem?

increase traffic but notes that "the city has not met its burden of demonstrating that the additional number of vehicle and bicycle trips generated by the petitioner's development reasonably relate to the city's requirement for a dedication of the pedestrian/bicycle pathway easement. . . . No precise mathematical calculation is required, but the city must make some effort to quantify its findings in support of the dedication . . . beyond the conclusionary statement that it could offset some of the traffic demand generated."[67] It is completely unclear how to implement the Court's order: estimates of the marginal number of car users that will come into town (especially at peak congestion hours) as a result of the store's expansion are guesswork at best, and estimates of the long-run impact of any bike path on car use, let alone a bike path that includes the land the developer must dedicate, are no better. The standard will likely be interpreted hyper-deferentially, given the realistic difficulties of quantification, but enormous costs will be borne developing extensive records.

While it may seem odd to argue that the Court should be satisfied with what might pejoratively be called a pleading requirement or an exercise in cleverness, the Court is in fact competent to do no more than ascertain whether there is a conceptual nexus between the exaction and the problems caused by development. In the takings area the Court generally is content to deal with conceptual issues rather than to try to perform a more substantive analysis of whether implicit or explicit tax burdens are fairly distributed. Thus, the Court finds a compensable taking when it finds that, conceptually, property interests are seized or possession taken—*Hodel, Loretto*—despite the fact that these seizures do not misdistribute tax burdens in any substantively significant way, and the Court looks quite loosely and deferentially at what might plausibly be seen as the maldistribution of tax burdens as long as the state engages in regulation. *Nollan* says that an exaction must be labeled as a regulation or a per se taking (property seizure), but since the line between per se takings and loosely reviewed regulations is itself conceptual and not based on a factual review of the effects of the regulation, it would seem unsurprising to find that the review of whether an exaction is a seizure or regulation should likewise be conceptual. The Court may be competent to do no more than say that a floodplain easement is logically related to paving and developing, just as it is competent to label the *Loretto* regulation as the seizure of physical possession.

---

67. 512 U.S. 374, 395–96 (1994).

*Dolan* is far worse than unadministerable, though. Demanding this sort of precision in exactions drives a needless wedge between the rules for regulation and the rules for exactions, driving the city to substitute regulations that are inferior from the vantage point of both the city and the developer for exactions. It is clear that the city could ban development on a general nonquantified showing that the development caused harm (congestion, flooding risk)—that is, the city would not have to show that the implicit tax levied by the development ban (the difference in market value of developed and undeveloped property) was proportional to the harm that would have been caused by development. (Some commentators writing right after *Nollan* was decided believed that the case signaled a marked increase in review of all economic regulations, demanding that the Court believe that the regulation was precisely tailored so that owners bore no more burdens than their own unregulated conduct would have caused,[68] but this view has simply not been sustained.) If the municipality is genuinely worried about flooding and congestion (i.e., this exaction, even if disproportionate, is not pretextual), it will ban the development if it cannot choose the Pareto-superior exaction route because the Court forbids it.

If the Court demands that despite its genuine concern about traffic or flooding, the city back off the demand for a bike path or greenway concession unless it can show that it receives no net benefits from either (i.e., that the bike path or greenway do no more than keep the city in the position it was in prior to development), the city will tend to take instead a step to which the Court will defer that obviously insures that the city stay in the position it was in prior to development (i.e., to ban development). The city will do so even if both it and the developer would prefer the exaction compromise. One interpretation of the rule the Court announces is that the city disgorge all net benefits—benefits in excess of harm caused—from a development exaction. The city would then be indifferent between a ban and an exaction unless it benefits from development itself. Given that the city will bear transaction costs in ascertaining net benefits and compensating owners, it will choose nondevelopment, even though it obviously would prefer

68. See, e.g., Nathaniel S. Lawrence, "Means, Motives, and Takings: The Nexus Test of *Nollan v. California Coastal Commission," Harvard Envtl. L. Rev.* 12 (1988): 231, 242–48, 253–59; "Comment, *First English Evangelical Lutheran Church of Glendale v. County of Los Angeles* and *Nollan v. California Coastal Commission:* The Big Chill," *Albany L. Rev.* 52 (1987): 325; Timothy A. Bittle, "*Nollan v. California Coastal Commission:* You Can't Always Get What You Want, but Sometimes You Get What You Need," *Pepperdine L. Rev.* 15 (1988): 345, 361–64.

the net benefit situation to the zero-development situation and the developer would obviously prefer development with exactions to nondevelopment.

The Court's response, I suspect, is that the city should be forced into electing between (otherwise undesirable from the city's vantage point) bans on development and general taxes when the nexus is insubstantial. When the nexus is insubstantial, the owner will argue, the city will not really ban the development just to meet its (by hypothesis trivial) interest in traffic and flood control. Since the city's real interest is in getting a bike path and greenway, the city will tax citizens generally and acquire those easements; since the city has no real interest in banning the development, it will not be banned. Thus, the city will move from exaction not to the (concededly less optimal) world of no development but to a more optimal one of development (modestly) tempered by real user fees and quasi-nuisance fines plus general taxes to fund recreational bike paths and general public-safety programs. The city's response, though, is that this outcome would occur if the exaction demands were pretextual but need not by any means occur whenever the city is a net beneficiary of the exaction (i.e., the city gets more benefits than it was harmed by development) but would actually be harmed by unconditional development.

Not only does *Dolan* force parties to bear high administrative costs of quantifying both the harms of development and the impact of the purported remedy and push local governments toward needless development bans, but any requirement to map conditions to problems caused by development on a parcel-by-parcel basis will lead to irrationally uncoordinated exactions. The basic underlying point is that if one is going to create a bike path, it must go in some sort of a gapless line (or bikes will need to fly). If one of the owners of property abutting the creek does not create enough extra traffic to justify seizing the bike path (given a precise quantification test), one still wants to demand that this owner fill in the bike path rather than make some other concession more specifically attributable to the changes caused by this particular development. The city is saying, in effect, that downtown development, broadly speaking, causes flood problems, traffic problems, loss of open space, and so on and that downtown developers can donate property in patterns that remedy these problems; however, tailoring each remedy to the particular problem without regard to the most economical form of concession is once more to force the city into "solutions" that harm everyone. Thus, the greenway/bike path concession may damage the owners of creek-abutting land rather little, while demanding that they purchase parkland because they have interfered with recreational areas or build viewing areas because they have harmed views may be constitutionally permitted (if there's a tighter nexus between these developments and view or park space loss) but worse for everyone involved.

Given the narrow reading of the exactions cases I have advanced here, the ADA's accommodation requirement almost surely does not raise an interesting takings issue. Owners simply cannot get past the first step of the analysis and show that what the state has demanded that they do to be free to operate their stores—provide greater access for those with mobility impairments—would constitute a taking if the state demanded such access without granting an explicit or implicit license[69] to operate a public accommodation.

Even if the owners did get past this first hurdle, their exactions claims would still fail: the government would meet its burden of saying that its easement seizure (assuming, for now, that it is so characterized) meets the same end as a valid regulation. The ADA proponents' claim would be most readily sustained if they were able to argue that the easement seizure substitutes for other regulations of public accommodation owners that permit those with disabilities to shop more readily (e.g., mandatory shopping assistants). In such a case, there would be a close fit between regulations that are permitted—cost-increasing demands for shopping aides— and a *Loretto* seizure that meets the same end.

In both *Nollan* and *Dolan,* of course, the regulation for which the easement seizures substituted was non-development, and it is a trickier question whether demanding access meets the same regulatory end as banning development of a nonaccessible store on the assumption that the existing exactions cases are read (narrowly) to ask simply whether the seized easement meets the same end as nondevelopment rather than the same end as any deferentially reviewed regulation.

The question of whether ADA access requirements meet the same end as nondevelopment becomes more unavoidable in the next chapter, which examines Justice Scalia's view, articulated at the intersection of the *Pennell* dissent and *Nollan,* that regulations can only legitimately avert exploitation or attempt to diminish or allocate social costs. But to preview the point I will raise in more detail, under one view, banning the store from

---

69. It is also by no means clear that the Court will extend the exactions analysis to encompass the more general, implicit permission granted by all jurisdictions to operate a concern if and only if one complies with relevant regulations.

opening would not serve the needs of the disabled community at all since if it were not open at all, no disabled patrons would have access to goods. In this view, the demand for the easement does not serve the same regulatory end as a ban would serve, since the ban serves no real end at all. But under an alternative view, which I find quite appealing, what those with disabilities seek, above all, is equality, and making the stores accessible to all is simply a more efficacious means of meeting the regulatory demand for equality. Nonaccessible stores would be banned from opening so that those with disabilities would not be excluded from the range of opportunities available to those without disabilities; that end can be met by making accessible the stores that do open.

CHAPTER 3

# Constitutional Considerations (II):
# A Less Deferential Alternative

In the first part of this chapter, I construct what I believe to be the most plausible theory of the Takings Clause that is less deferential to a governmental entity's decision to regulate rather than meet public aims through tax-and-spend programs.[1] I address at length the possibility that the Court will demand that governmental entities substitute broader-based taxes for regulations whose costs are borne by a narrower subgroup of citizens than a typical tax, and I address briefly the possibility that the Court should ban regulatory programs whose benefits are inadequately publicly dispersed even if it did not review parallel spending programs to insure such dispersion of benefits.

In the second part of this chapter, I argue that this, the most plausible interventionist theory of the Takings Clause, is ultimately unsatisfactory. It is readily recognized that the Court cannot, on the spending side, scrutinize whether programs are adequately public, in large part because there is no good theory, let alone one commanding constitutional consensus, differentiating programs that serve the public from those that serve coalitions of private parties. Understanding the fundamental interchangeability of regulation and taxation should make most people quickly realize that scrutinizing the implicit spending in regulatory programs for its publicness is an equally hopeless task.[2] I think it is more difficult to see at first blush but equally true that attacks on unduly narrowly based regulatory taxes

---

1. Again, when I describe this theory as plausible, I mean first that the Supreme Court is most likely to adopt this theory if adopting a more interventionist theory and second that while I ultimately find it seriously wanting, I believe it has more normative force than do other interventionist theories.

2. The Court decided in *Yee v. City of Escondido* to reach only the "physical seizure" (*Loretto*) issues rather than the issues raised by Judge Kozinski in *Hall v. City of Santa Barbara* that were dominant in the petitioner's brief. This decision reflected a recognition that detailed judicial scrutiny of whether the beneficiary class of regulations was an adequately dispersed or public group was not plausible.

assume, quite wrongly, that there is or should be activist constitutional scrutiny of unduly narrow explicit taxes.

## A First Statement of the Theory

I derive what I take to be the most plausible interventionist reading of the Takings Clause dominantly from my own interpretation of Justice Scalia's dissenting opinion in *Pennell* and his majority opinion in *Nollan,* but I do not claim that this reading is as faithful as one could be either to Justice Scalia's words or his intention. My point in this section is not to construct an interpretation faithful to an authoritative source. Thus, I will generally not cite particular passages in the cases that are most consistent with my reading unless they help explain an argument, nor will I attempt to deal with the passages that are least consistent with my reading. The basic argument is as follows:

1.   As I noted in the introductory chapter, it is vital to be aware that regulation and taxation are substitutes one for the other, whether or not they are permissible substitutes for one another.[3] The state almost invariably may meet its goals either through the public-spending programs that tax revenues finance or through regulatory mandates requiring that actors take certain steps and forbear from others. Private parties will treat regulatory mandates and explicit taxes as equivalents; to the extent that private parties are nonaltruistic, they are interested in the amount of goods they can privately appropriate, and that amount is the maximum gross income they could generate in a zero-tax, no-regulation world, net of the costs of compliance with either a tax or regulation.

2.   Governments are entitled to pursue two legitimate sorts of ends or goals. The Court will be extremely deferential to programs in either of these classes. First, the government is entitled to engage in regulation, and second, the government is entitled to engage in traditional tax-and-spend programs. Naturally, both these terms need workably clear definitions. Preliminarily, though, I would say that *regulation* consists first of efforts

---

3. I further noted in the introductory chapter that the state may choose to manage the same social problems that give rise to public-spending programs and/or regulation either by inaction (letting losses lie where they may unless private parties spontaneously choose to avert the losses) or by public provision of services for which those most benefited by the services must pay (user charges). The recognition that the state has these additional options, though, is germane to one critique of the interventionist position, not to its construction.

either to forbid activities, where doing so will result in limiting unwarranted social costs, or to force certain parties to compensate other parties that bear social costs. Second, *regulation* consists of efforts to insure that no party in a contractual relationship with another party exploits that party in any fashion either by unduly degrading the quality of the goods or services provided or by charging what might be thought to be an excessive price for the goods or services provided. Traditional tax-and-spend programs consist first of the provision of any good or service broadly consumed. The core cases might be spending programs in which the state entity provides what conventional public-finance economists would think of as goods that would be underconsumed in private markets. (For example, the state might provide pure public goods, like defense or protection of air quality, in which exclusion of beneficiaries from all the benefits of the spending is impossible, or goods whose consumption generates substantial positive externalities, like education or immunization, in which individuals capture some private exclusive benefits, but third parties cannot be excluded from capturing other gains.) The state may also publicly provide goods that largely lack these qualities. (For example, the state might provide health care of benefit only to sick people, which might be publicly provided dominantly for paternalistic reasons, or utility hookups, which almost exclusively help the particular dwellers who gain access to the relevant utility.) Second, traditional tax-and-spend programs may be redistributive. (State entities may choose to redistribute income in cash or, for paternalist or other reasons, in-kind. Typically, redistributive programs transfer income from richer to poorer individuals, but this is by no means necessarily the case. Redistributive transfers could go from one social group to another for a variety of reasons—for example, from the able-bodied to the disabled, from whites to African Americans, from nonveterans to veterans.)

3.   What the state is not permitted to do is to use regulation to meet one of the ends that has traditionally been accomplished and should continue to be accomplished through a tax-and-spend program. Operationally, though, the Court will not analyze what should be done through spending programs—recall that the Court in this conception is quite deferential to spending decisions and will therefore allow pretty much anything to be done through such programs, without a normative theory of their appropriate domain—but rather decide that a particular program is not a legitimate regulatory program. Generally, a regulation will be deemed to be ille-

gitimate when it is thought unfair to expect the regulated party rather than society at large to bear costs. Owners are bearing an unduly narrowly focused implicit tax unless they are asked to abate or pay for a social cost that they, along with the regulation's beneficiaries, are atypically responsible for creating or ordered to stop exploiting a contractual partner. There is a secondary argument that a regulation might be illegitimate because the benefits (implicit spending) of the program are inadequately publicly dispersed even though a parallel explicit spending program might be sustained.

### Illustrating the Application of the Theory: The *Pennell* Dissent, *Dolan,* and the ADA Case

(i) *Pennell, Nollan,* and *Dolan*

The San Jose municipal rent-control ordinance at issue in *Pennell* was an ordinary price-control measure with a single significant twist. One of the enumerated factors in determining the maximum rent that landlords could charge their tenants was the economic status of the tenant in possession. "Hardship" tenants might be entitled, by administrative order, to be charged lower rents than nonhardship tenants. Justice Scalia argued that this twist rendered the ordinance constitutionally suspect.[4]

Scalia himself doubtless believes that rent-control statutes are not just unwise policy but are premised on a misunderstanding of the workings of rental housing markets. Price controls, he believes, might be appropriate when sellers monopolize a market, but since the rental housing market is one with many sellers, he appears skeptical of the claims that rent control protects renters from exploitation.[5] However, he also believes that the legislature is entitled to regulate based on what he takes to be its incorrect belief that the market is monopolized and that the prices that landlords

---

4. *Pennell v. City of San Jose.*

5. Ibid., 20. ("The same cause-and-effect relationship [between the property use restricted by the regulation and the social evil that the regulation seeks to remedy] is popularly thought to justify emergency price regulation. When commodities have been priced at a level that produces exorbitant returns, the owners of these commodities can be viewed as responsible for the economic hardship that occurs. Whether or not that is an accurate perception of the way a free-market economy operates, it is at least true that the owners reap unique benefits from the situation.") For a strong argument that housing markets may not reach competitive equilibria despite the presence of large numbers of sellers, see Phillip Weitzman, "Economics and Rent Regulation: A Call for a New Perspective," *NYU Rev. of L. and Soc. Change* 13 (1984–85): 975.

charge tenants are therefore unjustly high. Given this supposition, a price regulation prevents the exploitation of the regulation's beneficiaries by the regulated party and is therefore valid.[6] Though the state entity would clearly have been permitted to substitute a tax-and-spend program for price regulation—collecting money from a broad base of taxpayers and transferring it (redistributively), whether in-kind (through housing vouchers) or cash, to those who could not afford market rates—it need not do so because the price-control program arguably serves a valid regulatory aim.

A program that controls rents only to the subset of hardship tenants, however, does not prohibit landlords from exploiting their tenants on some (misguided but constitutionally acceptable) theory that landlords are overcharging tenants. Instead, by not covering all tenants facing the same market conditions, the city implicitly concedes that it is not protecting buyers from exploitation but rather supplementing the income of a certain group of tenants.[7] If it is not protecting tenants from exploitation, though, it is using the regulation to accomplish an end that has been, and must, be accomplished through taxing and spending: the redistribution of income

---

6. *Pennell v. City of San Jose,* 20 (price regulation is valid when the seller causes the buyer's hardship).

7. This account of the city's intention is hardly unassailable. Imagine, for example, that San Jose is not the least bit interested in redistributing income to the poor but merely in efficiency: one can interpret this statute as directing monopolists to act as (imperfect) price discriminators, thus insuring that there are fewer efficiency losses associated with their monopoly power. If landlords charge uniform monopoly prices, some units will go unoccupied, though poorer (hardship) tenants would be able and willing to pay the cost—but not the price—of providing rental housing services. It is doubtful, though, that profit-maximizing landlords would have to be forced to lower prices rather than leave units vacant.

It is conceivable too, though in my mind nearly equally unpersuasive, to argue that the city believed that hardship tenants were more vulnerable to exploitation. My suspicion would be that even if poorer tenants are systematically less able to shop and/or bargain over rents, their poverty would make them less likely to pay more than the cost of provision of housing services than would richer tenants.

More plausibly, the city might well believe that it is difficult to resolve the question of whether landlords exploit their tenants when they charge them prevailing market rents in a tightening housing market. Given this ambiguity, the city chooses to split the difference, allowing landlords as a group to keep some but not all of what may be the monopoly profits that arise from scarcity. The city then chooses to protect only those most vulnerable to the seizure of scarcity rents. The question, to which I return in the text, is whether the city, in that case, should be forced to levy an excess-profits tax on all landlords and divide the proceeds among hardship tenants rather than to regulate those landlords renting to hardship tenants. At the same time, of course, it is necessary to ask whether a tax on all landlords is adequately broadly based, especially if there is uncertainty about whether it constitutes an excess-profits tax and the proceeds of the tax are earmarked for what appears in some senses to be a redistributive program.

(in-kind) to the poor.[8] The regulated party is no more responsible for the beneficiaries' poverty than are nonregulated parties.[9] The harm the program seeks to alleviate (poverty) is not the sort of harm (exploitation or the bearing of unwarranted social costs) regulation can justifiably alleviate.

That Scalia is willing to be deferential to legislative judgments not just that regulations preclude exploitation but that they avert unwarranted social costs can be seen both from his opinion in *Nollan* and from his refusal (thus far) to disclaim explicitly the *Penn Central* or *Miller v. Schoene* results. In *Nollan,* Scalia takes it for granted that the California Coastal Commission could have barred intensive shoreline development. Yet a prohibition on developing beachfront property would certainly not prevent a common law nuisance or any other traditional form of wrong-doing/harm-causing. Such a prohibition does, however, manage a social cost: the sum of the values of owning developable beachfront property and walking along the roads nearest a beach in a world in which the relevant activities (viewing the beach and ocean, developing the land) do not interact is clearly higher than their joint value in the world in which they do. Whether the social cost is most directly borne by the viewers (who cannot see the ocean when there is unfettered development) or the owner (who cannot build or must build differently or dedicate a viewing space to avoid interfering with the viewers' interest) is beside the point. It is constitutionally permissible for regulations to allocate such social costs.

Scalia, in this regard, accepts the argument that there is no bright-line distinction between regulation that averts harm and regulation that demands that parties confer benefits on others. The Court in *Miller v. Schoene*[10] certainly anticipates Coase's skepticism about the moral relevance of commonsensical causation judgments (while at the same time

---

Moreover, as I discuss later in the text, the idea that the state entity cannot define exploitation with an eye toward the specific character of the protected class is not especially persuasive: it is certainly possible to imagine a regulatory law protecting improvident buyers that required only those sellers who dealt with the impulsive or cognitively deficient to take costly steps to protect them from buying poorly. It may be similarly appropriate to define a fair pricing structure in part in terms of the capacity of the buyers with whom one deals.

8. Presumably, those following this theory would also seek to invalidate a number of parallel regulations that demand that providers subsidize the provision of certain services. Some such regulatory programs precisely parallel this one: for example, mandates during the energy crisis that utilities not raise fuel bills for senior citizens and impoverished customers.

9. An analogy may help: one may believe that a particular poor person should be able to buy more food than she currently can, but the grocer from whom she typically buys is not particularly responsible for her inability to buy all one thinks she should be able to buy.

10. 276 U.S. 272 (1928).

rejecting Scalia's Burkean/traditionalist reliance on the common law of nuisance that he employs in the limited *Lucas* class of cases) in declaring that ornamental red cedar tree owners may be forced, without compensation, to destroy their trees to prevent the spread of a rust disease that would otherwise infect nearby apple trees despite the fact that the cedar tree owners neither created a nuisance nor unambiguously harmed the apple tree owners. (Surely, it would be sensible to say that they were forced to destroy their own property to benefit the apple tree owners.)

In a Coasean world, causation judgments are arguably impossible—as Coase himself seems to have suggested—since each party is the but-for cause of the typical social harm. (Without the farmer's crops, there are no crop fires; without the train's emitted sparks, there are no crop fires.) Put like that, Coase's argument is true but morally obtuse: the fact that my having a nose—one of the two relevant but-for causes of my having a broken nose when you slug me—is not helpful in answering either ordinary questions of cause or, more significantly, moral responsibility. But Coase can be retranslated in a fashion that makes his views on causation more morally germane.[11] Typically, what must be accounted for in situations in which states choose to regulate, whether through nuisance law or statute, is a social cost—the cost that results from the fact that two activities must coexist, or, put more precisely, the difference in the sum of the values of the activities engaged in independently of one another and the sum of the values engaged in jointly. The social costs of spark-emitting trains running near flammable crop fields may be manifest in a wide variety of ways (crop fires; higher spark-suppressant costs; crops being grown further away from the tracks, thus lowering aggregate crop production). There may be a way of minimizing social cost (for example, spark suppressing may be cheaper or may be more expensive than moving crops back or tolerating the occasional fire), but there will be some social cost since crops could be grown on more land, without fires, or spark suppressants avoided if these activities did not abut or inhabit the same social world. But the social cost is not in any apparent sense either party's moral responsibility (unless one party's consumption desire morally trumps the other party's), nor is it possible to say which party physically caused the social cost (if it is manifest as fire, it might be caused by sparks; if it is manifest as spark suppressant, it might be caused by the farmer's placement of his crops).

The owner's claim in *Dolan* is that the floodplain greenway and bike

---

11. See Mark Kelman, "Necessary Myth," 579, 581–86.

path are general public projects that should be purchased, using general tax revenues, from the relevant landowners, except to the degree that the need for them is caused specifically by the owner's development. Developers may, though they need not, be asked to bear social costs (increasing the risk of flooding; increasing car use with its negative impacts on traffic flow, air quality, and so on), whether by being forced to restrict development or by an exaction that meets the same end, which amounts to charging an in-kind fee for being one of the parties jointly responsible for creating a social cost. Presumably, too, developers could be asked to fund programs that specifically benefit them (a user fee/benefit tax is once again permitted, though seemingly not mandated). But to the extent that the city of Tigard cannot establish that it is simply forcing developers to bear the social costs associated with development or pay for a project of atypical benefit to them, developers cannot be singled out to pay any more to fund the public improvement than any other "similarly situated citizen."[12]

## (ii) The ADA Case

Federal regulatory officials could not, given this conception of the Takings Clause, unambiguously defend the requirement that people who (happen to be?) owners of public accommodations bear the costs of making their facilities accessible to customers with disabilities. The statute is clearly defensible given current practice norms, because even those regulations requiring the dedication of certain portions of the property to improve accessibility do not seize title or transfer a traditional property right to the third party beneficiaries of the regulation. However, if this more interventionist perspective were adopted, the Court would have to ask: (a) whether public accommodation owners can be singled out either as injuring the disabled or at least partly creating a social cost by their proposed conduct, and (b) whether the fact that the regulation applies to public accommodation owners generally rather than some subgroup of owners makes what might be treated as an implicit tax adequately broadly based. My sense is that the theory, rigorously applied, might well demand that the federal government compensate owners forced to comply with many, though not all, of the ADA's reasonable accommodation requirements. At the same

---

12. The phrase *similarly situated citizen* appears in quotation marks precisely because it is so problematic: I argue later in the chapter that there is no reasonable constitutional theory to label the dimensions along which citizens must be similarly situated when they are taxed explicitly, and therefore there should be no such theory when they are taxed implicitly.

time, I suspect that the recognition that such is the case would give considerable pause to many people who might otherwise be drawn to the theory stated in the abstract or even applied to cases like *Dolan.*

(a) Does the access requirement meet a permissible regulatory end?

It is most helpful, I think, in doing this analysis, to think of the ADA's accommodation requirements as establishing a scheme of exactions. The exaction analogy is reasonably straightforward: in exchange for the right to start (or continue to operate) a business classed as a public accommodation, owners must agree to provide greater access to those with disabilities than the owners would choose to do in the absence of the regulation, given the costs of so doing and the legal and practical barriers to recovering these costs by charging disabled customers the incremental cost of the accommodation. (Recall that this supposition applies only to cases in which the owner bears some genuine cost in accommodating. The ADA is clearly premised in some significant part on what strikes me as the justifiable supposition that owners often wrongly believe that making facilities accessible will be costly when doing so is not. Opponents of the ADA often argued that the statute would prove extremely financially burdensome, especially for small business employers.[13] Studies seem to reveal, though, that the costs of accommodating disabled employees have in fact generally been quite low.)[14]

What differentiates exaction law in this expansive theory and the actual law dealing with exactions that I detailed in chapter 2 is simply that current law applies only in situations in which the municipality exacts title from the owner. In this more expansive and interventionist view, though, aspects of existing law are used to identify cases in which a regulation does not really serve a traditional regulatory end.

---

13. See, e.g., Thomas H. Barnard, "The Americans with Disabilities Act: Nightmare for Employers and Dream for Lawyers?" *St. John's Law Rev.* 64 (1990): 229, 251–52, and George C. Dolatly, "The Future of the Reasonable Accommodation Duty in Employment Practices," *Columbia J. of L. and Soc. Problems* 26 (1993): 523, 546 (both arguing that the ADA places an onerous financial burden, including litigation costs, on employers).

14. See, e.g., "Developments in the Law: Employment Discrimination," *Harvard L. Rev.* 109 (1996): 1568, 1619–20 (noting that studies indicate that the average cost of accommodation is less than one thousand dollars and as low as two hundred dollars per employee, that some employers have even reported savings as a result of accommodating their disabled employees, and that the costs of accommodation are lower than the costs of litigation).

It is also helpful to imagine two distinct sorts of regulatory requirements. In the first class of cases, the accommodation requirements apply only prospectively[15] but order owners not only to design buildings to be as accessible as possible to those with disabilities, if choosing between two equally profitable buildings, but also to accommodate even when doing so is (not unreasonably) costly.[16] Imagine, second, that the ADA applies both prospectively and retroactively, demanding retrofitting efforts (as long as they do not cost an unreasonable amount). Within this second class of cases, it can be imagined that only some of the firms that need to retrofit made non-cost-based decisions in the past that were detrimental to the interests of those with disabilities.[17]

It would be difficult, but perhaps not impossible, to find, as one must under *Nollan,* that this regulation serves the same permissible end that a ban on development (or a ban on allowing a business to continue to operate) would serve or to interpret *Dolan* and *Nollan* somewhat less precisely to argue that this exaction does no more than rectify the problem that the owner's development causes.[18] At first blush, the regulatory aim, to insure that people with disabilities have access to a range of goods and services, would not be met by a development ban. If the store does not exist at all, it offers people with, for example, certain mobility impairments no more goods and services than if it exists without ramps. In that sense, since the regulation does not substitute for a development ban, it is impermissible. Similarly, the argument would be that development of nonaccessible facil-

---

15. Accommodation requirements for mass-transit providers are more stringent prospectively than retrospectively. Thus, for example, a commuter railroad could not purchase any new equipment that was inaccessible to those who use wheelchairs but need not make wheelchair-accessible more than one car per existing train. See P.L. 101–306, §242(b)(1), §242(b)(2)(A), and §242(c). Similarly, providers of intercity railroad services had twenty years to make existing stations accessible, although new stations could not be built that were not accessible to those with disabilities. Compare §242(e)(1) with §242(e)(2)(A)(ii)(I).

16. It is probably easiest to think about this sort of accommodation if one considers something other than an environmental modification, even though takings law is generally associated with the exaction of real property rather than fees or services. Imagine that any law firm that opens after the effective date of the ADA, but none that opened before, must insure that hearing-impaired clients can communicate with the lawyers, at firm expense, by providing interpreters facile in signing.

17. For example, they may have chosen to install an inaccessible stairway over a ramp although it did not decrease costs or increase available floor space. Other firms, though, are like those covered by the prospective provisions. They are simply asked to bear the unavoidably higher costs of serving certain customers with disabilities.

18. In most cases, including this one, I don't think the formulations are distinct. See chapter 2, text following n. 61, for an explanation of why I generally prefer the first formulation.

ities itself does not cause or add to a problem—lack of access to goods and services—but simply leaves the situation as it was prior to development. In *Dolan*'s terms, this exaction puts the governmental entity in a better position than it was prior to development, which is impermissible. The exaction must do no more than make the regulator indifferent between development and nondevelopment, at least as long as the exaction could be made less onerous for developers. Yet another way of getting at this same point is that one would generally believe, at first blush, that the interaction of disabled customers and a nonaccessible store does not decrease the wealth of either party compared to the interaction of a disabled customer with no store at all. In this view, the accommodation requirement can seemingly be justly imposed on only one class of owners: those who must retrofit because their initial design decisions disadvantaged those with disabilities but did not save real social resources. Such parties could be said to have decreased the chances that disabled people would have access to facilities, since scale economies in service provision make it less likely that an accessible provider of the same service will come along after the inaccessible facility is built.

The best argument that the ADA is constitutionally permissible if uncompensated regulations are reviewed in this fashion would appear to be that a ban on building nonaccessible facilities would, in fact, meet a regulatory goal. If the regulatory goal is not simply to increase access to goods and services but to insure equality of access to goods and services or the absence of exclusion from activities available to the able, then the access requirement could be said, alternatively, to substitute for a development ban or remedy the problem of unequal access toward which the creation of new inaccessible facilities contributes. (Similarly, the creation of the public accommodation creates a social cost from an access equality perspective. The wealth—commodifying all subjective end states—of the class of disabled persons is diminished by the presence of inaccessible facilities below the level that existed when there were simply no facilities, just as either Coase's farmers are less wealthy once spark-emitting railroads are nearby or the railroads are less wealthy when they must interact with fire-vulnerable farmers.) The argument seems rather compelling that at least a purpose, if not the sole purpose, of regulations mandating access is to avoid the sociopsychological harms that result from being marked as a social outsider or lacking the sense of belonging that one can get only if integrated into whatever a community's ordinary social life may be. It is also important to recall that in my view, this general theory of the Takings

Clause is quite deferential to regulatory programs. Thus, the ban would likely be sustained even though development of nonaccessible facilities is clearly not a traditional tort toward the disabled and does not unambiguously harm them.

A court adopting this theory would still be faced with a *Dolan* problem, though. If there must be some rough proportionality between what the state gets through this regulation (both physical access to goods and services and social inclusion as equals for the population with disabilities) and what it would get through the development ban (merely social inclusion as equals), some might interpret *Dolan* as mandating that the state disgorge the net benefits either by disclaiming the regulation or by compensating owners for the losses borne to create the net benefits. I believe such a view is unpersuasive, even if one reads *Dolan* expansively. *Dolan* does not preclude uncompensated regulation in this case because the governmental entity took no more than was needed to undo the negative impact (inequality of participation) of development. The fact that the state happened to get additional benefits (physical access to goods) does not by itself render the regulation suspect. In *Dolan* itself, in this view, the problem is that the state simply did not need a public greenway to deal with flooding or this particular bike path to deal with traffic congestion. There is no reason to believe, though, that the Court would or should have invalidated the exaction of the bike easement if it precisely remedied the congestion problem caused by the store's expansion just because city officials were also glad that it permitted, for example, better views of the creek for recreational bicyclists than they had had in the past.

(b) If this is a tax rather than a legitimate regulation, is it adequately broad based?

When I return to criticize the viability of this general theory of constitutional review, I will highlight the point that the theory as developed up until now has not, and in my view could not, answer the question of whether any tax, explicit or implicit, is levied on a constitutionally permissible base. It is clear that a permissible general tax must treat equally some group of individuals who are similarly situated along some relevant dimension, but it is not clear how many people must be in the group or along what dimensions equality may be measured. For now, though, I will make three different points.

First, it is possible that judges utilizing this theory of review would simply decide that a regulation covering all American public accommodations is adequately broad, simply because such a large number of implicit taxpayers are affected by the regulation. The sorts of exactions that have typically been litigated have affected single parties—that is, literally no parties other than the plaintiff have been asked to pay (implicitly) the precise same tax that the owner has been asked to pay. It is conceivable that the theory restricts only regulatory taxes applied to individuals or small groups.

Second, it is possible that the ADA would be constitutionally impermissible given this theory of review if applied only prospectively. However, an implicit tax that put new and old businesses in the same position as each other (expecting each to spend whatever it takes, within reason, to solve the access problem) might be administratively senseless since it might demand that old businesses waste more resources on retrofitting, given the contributions such expenditures make to genuine access. It is not clear in the *Dolan* context, for example, whether it would have been permissible to demand that all downtown businesses contribute to a bike path, even if one believed that the businesses do not cause a congestion problem the path can alleviate, on the ground that a uniform tax on downtown businesses is adequately broad based. (It is not clear because none of the cases have, or in my mind could, specify when a base is adequately broad.) But it is clear that the Court believes the base is unduly narrow when it applies only to those businesses applying for building permits—that is, those that are either opening or expanding businesses. A prospective ADA, though, in essence, establishes a federal building permit system: it applies a regulatory requirement only to those who seek to build new facilities (new businesses or expanding old businesses), allowing permission (a form of federal license) to operate the business to turn on meeting access demands. (At the substantive level, I take it, proponents of this form of review believe they are protecting certain insular or identifiable minorities from expropriation by the broader group; as the expropriated parties themselves become adequately broad based, this problem becomes less of a concern. The fear, then, in *Dolan,* is that coalitions of relatively indifferent taxpayers and old businesses impose all the costs of meeting certain general social goals on isolated new businesses, plucking them off one at a time when they seek permits. But it is hard to see why a federal program that plucks off new businesses several thousand at a time while immunizing hundred of thousands more old businesses from requirements to contribute to meeting some social problem is really much better.)

Third, and perhaps most significant, it is possible that the ADA's reasonable accommodation requirement as it is usually interpreted—demanding higher expenditures to accommodate the disabled by those entities able to afford the expenditures on the supposition that an accommodation requirement is unreasonable only when it threatens the viability of the accommodating institution—is unconstitutional under this theory because an entity's profitability has nothing to do with whether it injures those with disabilities by opening or operating nonaccessible facilities. If, instead, the idea behind levying a higher implicit tax on hyperprofitable firms is to tax those whose tax-paying capacity is high, there appears to be little reason, within this conception of the Takings Clause, to single out those well-heeled taxpayers who happen to operate public accommodations. Just as the tenant's hardship does not change the degree to which a landlord exploits the tenant in Scalia's view of the San Jose rent-control ordinance at issue in *Pennell,* so owners' wealth or capacity to increase accessibility do not affect the degree to which those with disabilities are harmed by the failure to provide certain sorts of access.

## Critiquing the Interventionist Theory: A First Statement of the Primary Critique

If it is correct to say that explicit taxing-and-spending programs could substitute for regulations, it may well be the case that the constitutional limits on regulation can be no more stringent than the constitutional limits on taxation or spending.

This point appears relatively uncontroversial when the focus is on the implicit spending side. Many believe it might be valuable to make implicit spending decisions more politically transparent by forbidding regulations that serve unduly private ends; the instinct behind that belief is that narrow constituencies should receive government largesse only when it is explicitly appropriated to them, when the funds expended for their benefit are clearly marked on budget. But the proponents of such increased transparency have justifiably been quite unsuccessful in gaining adherents to the view that it might be constitutionally mandated to review regulatory programs for publicness more stringently than explicit spending programs.

Take the mobile-home-pad rent-control statutes that were the subject of litigation in both *Yee* and *Hall.* Attacks on both the California state statute (which permitted local rent control, barred mobile-home-park owners from charging transfer fees on the sale of a mobile home, and precluded park owners from rejecting mobile-home buyers as tenants without good reasons) and the local ordinance, which limited rents that could be charged to mobile-home-pad occupants, take the following tack: First, they concede that conventional rent control is constitutional. When land available for housing or a particular kind of housing is scarce (i.e., its supply is essentially fixed), whether because growth in demand outstrips supply responsiveness or because municipal zoning precludes supply expansion (as it almost certainly does in the case of mobile-home parks), it is permissible to control prices to prevent the transfer of consumer surplus to effective monopolists. Rent-control statutes prevent this transfer by setting prices and forbidding would-be occupants to bid up the price of housing to market rates. Any current occupant benefits (at least in the short run) from such a program. This state and local mobile-home price-control scheme, though, does not protect occupants from paying market rents. The public regulatory interest in protecting occupants from exploitation by monopolists is legitimate, but it will not be met here. To occupy a mobile home, one must both rent a pad and purchase a mobile home that sits on the pad, since there are effectively no empty pads available for new mobile homes to occupy. Though rent for the pad is set by the rent-control statute, those willing to pay more to rent the pad will simply bid more to purchase the mobile homes. Thus, assume the market value of the mobile home is thirty thousand dollars and the market rent is five thousand dollars per year, but rent control restricts market rent to two thousand dollars per year. Buyers willing to pay five thousand dollars per year rent will simply pay far more than thirty thousand dollars for a home; they will pay that amount plus the value of the right to occupy the pad for three thousand dollars a year less than the rent they would be willing to pay (and the right to convey that same right to a third purchaser). In essence, the price of the pad is uncontrolled; it is simply the case that the tenants in possession at the time the rent-control ordinance passes rather than the park owners receive (the discounted present value of) the difference between the controlled and market prices.

Even assuming, solely for argument's sake, that occupying tenants are not protected from paying monopoly profits and that only tenants in possession at the time of the passage of the statute gain from it, should the statute be invalidated?[19] Mobile-home-park owners claim that this scheme

---

19. For a different view of the statutory purpose that focuses on the degree to which the state and local statutory schemes in combination protected tenants against the expropriation of their site-specific investments, given the especially high explicit and implicit moving costs for mobile-home-pad renters, see AFL-CIO's amicus curiae brief in support of the respondent, *Yee v. City of Escondido* (no. 90–1947).

serves only to transfer the right to receive monopoly profits from the landlord to the tenants in possession at the time of the enactment of the statute and that this transfer constitutes a redistribution to particular private parties rather than to some group that can be identified in terms of any publicly cognizable status. The statute does not protect occupants from high housing prices but simply redirects occupants' housing payments from the owner to a group of private parties and thus serves to fulfill no public goal. While *Poletown Neighborhood Council v. City of Detroit*[20] is typical of state court holdings that do not invalidate any scheme from which private parties (like General Motors) benefit, and *Hawaii Housing Authority v. Midkiff,* at the federal level, explicitly allows redistribution to land tenants in possession to reduce the concentration of landownership, such cases arguably require that the legislature might at least believe that others, besides the most direct beneficiaries, may benefit as well from the taking (e.g., through economic growth in *Poletown* or some combination of increased social integration and less monopolistic housing prices in *Midkiff*). Naked transfers of monopoly rents have no public purpose.

Certainly, though, a public spending program that transferred taxpayer funds to occupants in possession at the time the ordinance was passed would be permissible, whether the transfer occurred through a tax abatement for such current occupants (à la Proposition 13, whose constitutionality was upheld in *Nordlinger v. Hahn*)[21] or through direct funds transfers to such occupants. The claim that this transfer is permissible if enacted directly but not if enacted via regulation must be no more than a prudential claim about the political-process perils of invisible transfers, because visible transfers to what some might quite reasonably identify as particular constituencies are unquestionably constitutionally unproblematic.[22]

Courts must, given current understandings of what "public" goals are, approach both ordinary spending programs and the public-use requirement in takings law quite deferentially. The distinction between true public purposes and aggregated private purposes is too conceptually blurry to provide a basis for critiquing particular programs. Many in this

---

20. 304 N.W. 2d 455 (1981).

21. 505 U.S. 1 (1992).

22. I will address later in this chapter and in chapter 5 what I see as the limited persuasiveness of the argument that, in some general sense, implicit transfers are less transparent and hence less subject to democratic scrutiny than are explicit transfers.

political culture believe there can be no transcendent public purposes, that all public programs simply aggregate private purposes and interests. Those who adhere to this view believe, in fact, that this is a necessary truth (since they believe that only individuals rather than collectivities can have interests or purposes). Even the most traditional public programs (in terms of history and public-finance economists' pedigree) meet some individuals' aims better than others: roads help drivers more than nondrivers; defense expenditures protect those in areas more vulnerable to attack more than those in isolated rural locations; those receiving subsidized public education privately capture at least some substantial portion of the gains from education.

Naturally, then, the state and municipality should argue that even if the redistribution occurred entirely to those tenants who happened to be in possession at the time the ordinance was enacted, that outcome is legitimate. The legal point is doubtless grounded in the minimalism of the *Poletown/Midkiff* public-purpose requirement, but I believe there is a more powerful if less legally familiar argument to be made. The owners' constitutional claim to void a scheme giving tenants in possession control of the monopoly rents ought to be no better than the constitutional claim of the tenants in possession against the traditional property regime that permitted the owners to retain monopoly rents. Absent some sort of natural rights perspective, the ownership of the monopoly rents is simply up for grabs (particularly, but by no means exclusively, since the monopoly rents were in substantial part created by the state through its restrictive zoning decisions), and if the state even mildly prefers that tenants in possession (who may be marginally poorer or who may have claims as old-timers) get the monopoly rents, the decision is valid.

It is perhaps less obvious that the same problem plagues the implied-tax side. In the absence of a more thought-out view of the constitutionally permissible explicit tax bases,[23] it is difficult to know when a particular implicit tax is unduly narrow. There are remarkably few constitutional limits on the breadth of explicit taxes. Proponents of the view that regulations should never substitute for more legitimate explicit general taxes must recognize that regulations may function as legitimate taxes.

---

23. None of the obvious conventional bases (income, consumption, property ownership) are constitutionally mandated, and they should not be. I will subsequently discuss why sales taxes, if they exist, need not be uniformly levied on all commodities and the implications of that fact for thinking generally about constitutionalizing tax bases.

**The Tax-Base Problem**

Assume that the hardware store owner asked to donate land or money (and for my purposes it does not matter which) to build a bike path in a case like *Dolan* in exchange for a building permit is indeed bearing a tax to fund what is *arguendo* a nonregulatory program benefiting the general public. Imagine that the store owner pays one or more other local taxes: taxes levied on the assessed value of his property, a sales tax on items that he purchases, maybe even a local income tax. He claims that he pays more than other citizens who are equal along all relevant dimensions (presumably, given the hypothetical town's tax system, these dimensions are property ownership, consumption of taxable goods, and income) because he alone is asked to pay an additional tax when he seeks a building permit to expand his premises. Why would such a tax be considered illegitimate? How would it be determined that he had been singled out to bear a burden that should be borne by taxpayers generally rather than identified as someone who owed more taxes? How would the court declare that he was similarly situated along all relevant dimensions yet treated differently when he was clearly dissimilar along a dimension the local government declared relevant? If the locality argues that what differentiates the store owner from those who pay lower taxes is that the others were not applying for a building permit, what is the interventionist court to answer? There are two broad ways to answer that question. First, existing practice can be used to determine when an explicit tax could be challenged, successfully, on equal protection grounds. Second, a standard less deferential to explicit and implicit tax allocation decisions can be imagined.

(i) Equal Protection and Taxation: A Picture of
Near-Total Deference

No scheme that classifies taxpayers differently based on some fact about their situation will be invalidated under current law on equal-protection grounds, except in four sorts of cases. Unless tax classifications are based on status, burden the exercise of a protected constitutional right (e.g., free speech, the right to travel across the states), discriminate against out-of-staters, or are administered by officials in plain violation of express state policy, review will be highly deferential: "If the selection or classification is neither capricious nor arbitrary, and rests upon some reasonable consideration of definition of policy, there is no denial of equal protection of the laws."[24] None of the implicit regulatory taxes examined here suffers from these defects. While it is plausible that some exactions incidentally burden newcomers, the fact that they apply on their face equally to out-of-state and in-state developers would probably preclude challenges focusing on either the right to travel or Commerce Clause–like concerns.

Courts have upheld all sorts of classifications that tax persons differently depending on factors distinct from their wealth, income, spending, or owner-ship of equally valuable resources. A state may, for example, tax personal property held by a corporation more than identical personal property held by the same sort of business conducted in noncorporate form[25] or exempt veter-ans groups but not other nonprofit lobbying organizations, from certain taxes.[26] Most interestingly, in thinking about the sorts of regulatory taxes of which Scalia is so suspicious in *Pennell,* an explicit New York tax levied against utilities but not other businesses, for the benefit of unemployment relief gener-ally, was upheld in *New York Rapid Transit Corp. v. City of New York.*[27]

Tax classifications are overturned in very few circumstances. If a tax were to classify persons in terms of an ascriptive status, whether a status distinction subject to strict scrutiny (like race) or intermediate scrutiny (like gender), the tax regulation would then be reviewed like any other such status-conscious government enactment. Thus, just as a preference in benefits grants to widows over widowers has been overruled when based on irrational stereotypes,[28] so a property tax that exempted widows would pass muster only if it relied not on archaic and overly broad generaliza-tions about women but data about the impact of spousal loss on members of each gender.[29] Second, if people's taxpaying obligations varied in ways that burdened the exercise of a constitutional right, the tax statute would be reviewed like any other piece of legislation so burdening the right.[30]

---

24. *Allied Stores of Ohio, Inc. v. Bowers,* 358 U.S. 522, 527 (1985).

25. *Lenhauer v. Lake Shore Auto Parts Co.,* 410 U.S. 356 (1973).

26. *Regan v. Taxation with Representation of Washington,* 461 U.S. 540 (1983).

27. 303 U.S. 573 (1938), rehearing denied 304 U.S. 588 (1938).

28. See, e.g., *Califano v. Goldfarb,* 430 U.S. 199 (1977) (striking down Social Security pro-vision that provided benefits to all widows of deceased workers but provided benefits for wid-owers of deceased workers only if the widower had been receiving at least half his support from his deceased wife).

29. See *Kahn v. Shevin,* 416 U.S. 351, 355–56 (1974) (upholding such a statute). The cases may not be distinguishable in fact, and it is unclear whether *Kahn* survives *Goldfarb,* or, at a minimum, is restricted to its facts.

30. See, e.g., *Minneapolis Star & Tribune Co. v. Minn. Comm'r. of Revenue,* 460 U.S. 575 (1983) (a special-use tax applicable only to print media is a presumptive violation of Free Speech guarantees).

Third, and most commonly, equal-protection norms are invoked to find that states may not ordinarily tax out-of-staters more than state residents by virtue of that fact alone,[31] just as states cannot distribute benefits to longtime residents not available to those arriving more recently.[32] These decisions, even when grounded explicitly in the Equal Protection Clause, appear to have far less to do with equality concerns than with the desire both to protect citizens' right to travel among the states and to insure that a single national market is maintained. Fourth, and finally, local officials may not distinguish arbitrarily between two taxpayers, in the limited sense that the officials are acting arbitrarily if the distinctions, though defensible as a matter of abstract policy, are not distinctions that the state has directed be made: thus, county officials in West Virginia cannot reassess property only when it is sold when the state constitution directs that property be evaluated according to current market value,[33] even

---

31. See, e.g., *Hooper v. Bannadillio County Assessor,* 472 U.S. 612 (1985) (New Mexico could not allocate property-tax exemptions only to the subset of Vietnam War veterans who had lived in state prior to 1976, though the allocation of such benefits to veterans or even in-state veterans did not itself pose problems); *Metropolitan Life Ins. Co. v. Ward,* 470 U.S. 869, 880 (1985) (state cannot, consistent with the Equal Protection Clause, tax out-of-state insurance companies more than in-state companies); *William v. Vermont,* 472 U.S. 14, 23–24 (1985) (state cannot, consistent with the Equal Protection Clause, give residents who bought cars out of state credit against an auto-use tax for sales tax paid on cars purchased out of state without giving the same credit to nonresidents who purchased cars now being driven in Vermont).

32. See *Zobel v. Williams,* 457 U.S. 55 (1982) (Alaska cannot constitutionally distribute a higher portion of state oil-lease revenues to longtime residents).

33. *Allegheny Pittsburgh Coal Co. v. Webster County,* 488 U.S. 336, 345 (1989). It is worth noting that the Court may have incorrectly discredited or misunderstood the county assessor's claim that reevaluating property in the absence of sale was not feasible: the complaint that properties with equal market values were taxed differently may have ignored the fact that it was difficult to value land that looks comparable but might or might not contain commercially exploitable quantities of coal. As soon as such coal was discovered, the land was sold; in the absence of sale, the land was simply assumed to be noncomparable (whether or not it had coal, the land was less valuable because people did not yet know it had coal). See Robert Jerome Glennon, "Taxation and Equal Protection," *George Washington L. Rev.* 58 (1990): 261, 271–72.

It also may seem odd to allow a finding that the Equal Protection Clause is violated to turn on whether the government official is violating the state's own law. As Cohen has noted, guarantees of equality should apply equally to official state policies and eccentric administrative practices. See William Cohen, "State Law in Equality Clothing: A Comment on *Allegheny Pittsburgh Coal Company vs. County Commission,*" *UCLA L. Rev.* 38 (1990): 87, 92–93. The Court's ostensible explanation—that the Court simply follows state authorities in interpreting relevant local law and is thus deciding a case given a record in which the state has disclaimed reliance on any of the ends that might plausibly differentiate the taxpayers' status—may be inadequate; the result might instead have been driven by the peculiar absence of relevant state law remedies for the violation of the state's own taxing laws. See John Hart Ely, "Another Spin on *Allegheny Pittsburgh,*" *UCLA L. Rev.* 38 (1990): 107, 110.

though the state of California can constitutionally mandate that property be assessed only when it is acquired rather than at market value.[34]

It is plausible, though not clear, that an entity could not impose a tax or surcharge on a named or readily identified party.[35] Obviously, the distinction between exemptions and surcharges is not going to be clean. Where a municipality has granted property tax abatements to most but not all businesses in the jurisdiction, the failure to extend such abatements to all would not as a formal matter impose a surcharge or nongeneral tax on the nonexempted entities but would produce a result that was indistinguishable in substance. There appears to be no case law barring such a practice, however.

## (ii) What More Interventionist Accounts of Permissible Tax Bases Might and Might Not Plausibly Look Like

If the Court concludes that a regulated party may in some cases be overpaying when asked to bear an implicit tax, the Court must decide that the party is unjustly taxed because it is equal to others less heavily taxed in relationship to some base. But what base is constitutionally mandated? It is clear that income is not the only permissible base: thus, the fact that the owner pays more taxes than other citizens with his precise income will not, by itself, mean that he has been unjustly taxed. As a matter of history, very few municipalities and relatively few states have employed income taxes; the federal government raises a great deal of revenue from sources other than the personal income tax, and did so to an even greater extent until well into the twentieth century. As a matter of policy, many

---

34. *Nordlinger v. Hahn,* 505 U.S. 1 (1992) (upholding California's Proposition 13 despite the fact that the complainant paid property taxes more than five times as high as those levied against neighbors with identically valuable homes, because the state could plausibly defend such a program as helpful to preserving neighborhood stability and protecting reasonable reliance interests). The *Allegheny Pittsburgh Coal* Court had anticipated *Nordlinger,* noting, "we need not and do not decide today whether the Webster County assessment method would stand on a different footing if it were the law of a state instead of the aberrational enforcement policy it appears to be" (488 U.S. 336, 344 n. 4).

35. A governmental entity can clearly exempt a particular taxpayer from regulations, even if that party is named. See *New Orleans v. Duke,* 427 U.S. 297, 306 (1976), explicitly overruling *Doud v. Morey,* 354 U.S. 457 (1957), which had held that regulations against the issuance of money orders that exempted American Express, by name, violated the Equal Protection Clause. A government can certainly exempt taxpayers who are clearly identifiable though formally unnamed.

economists believe that income is a poor base, either for extrinsic reasons[36] or for fairness reasons.[37]

It is more interesting still, keeping in mind the focus on exactions, to consider owners' types of claims in a jurisdiction that raised all money through a selective sales tax (e.g., one that exempted certain household items or set rates especially high for certain status-oriented luxuries). Presumably, some would argue that a selective sales tax is unfair because it taxes those with the same aggregate consumption differently. Why, the taxpayer might ask, should I pay more taxes because I use less household detergent but take clothes to the cleaners or buy more expensive clothes? Plainly, though, a selective sales tax is constitutional. The municipality's decision to tax certain items and not others is unassailable even though it will unquestionably result in differentiating the burdens some people bear on the basis of a factor other than income or aggregate consumption. (To anticipate an argument, to which I will return later, that the Court should

---

36. The use of an income rather than consumption tax base arguably causes serious welfare losses. For standard arguments to that effect, see, e.g., Martin Feldstein, "The Welfare Cost of Capital Income Taxation" *J. Pol. Econ.* 86 (1978): S29; Lawrence H. Summers, "Capital Taxation and Accumulation in a Life Cycle Growth Model," *Am. Econ. Rev.* 71 (1981): 533; Michael J. Boskin, "Taxation, Saving, and the Rate of Interest" *J. Pol. Econ.* 86 (1978): S3.

37. Compared to a consumption tax, an income tax may overtax a subset of those people with identical productive capacity who defer consumption, and market-realized productive capacity may well be a reasonable base in some views. For critical discussions of the claim that the income tax is fairer than a consumption tax that exempts savings, see, e.g., Barbara Fried, "Fairness and the Consumption Tax," *Stanford L. Rev.* 44 (1992): 961; Mark Kelman, "Time Preference and Tax Equity," *Stanford L. Rev.* 34 (1983): 649. Conventional attacks on the equity of the income tax are presented in, e.g., William Andrews, "A Consumption-Type or Cash Flow Personal Income Tax," *Harvard L. Rev.* 87 (1974): 1113, 1167–69; U.S. Department of the Treasury, *Blueprints for Basic Tax Reform* (Washington, DC: U.S. Government Printing Office 1977), 38–42. Still others may believe that it is just to tax people on what they have taken out of the common pool (private preclusive consumption) rather than what they have created (earnings). See, e.g., Andrews, *id.,* 1165–67. Other people believe that a benefits tax is most appropriate and that income is a poor surrogate for the degree to which one benefits from government services.

Similarly, while local governments have most typically relied on taxing those who own equal amounts of real property equally, it is quite clear that a claim that one must be protected by the Court because one was taxed more than others owning equal amounts of real property hardly seems constitutionally compelling. More tellingly, the Court (in a decision that Justice Scalia joined) has tolerated local decisions to tax owners of real property differently from one another depending on when they purchased the property. See *Nordlinger v. Hahn.* It seems less than intuitively obvious that it is constitutionally permissible to say that taxpayers are treated adequately equally as long as all those who bought property after a certain date are taxed equally, even if those who bought before that date pay a lower percentage of market value in taxes, but not permissible to say that taxpayers are treated equally as long as all those seeking building permits are equally taxed.

attempt to prevent majorities from imposing taxes on identifiable parties, knowing that the majorities will not be subject to the levies, one should note that there would seem to be no possibility of challenging a selective sales tax even though the legislative majority could or did know what sub-group of the population was likely to bear the predominant burden of the tax. Imagine high sales taxes on recreational boats or private club memberships in a jurisdiction where virtually all consumers of such items are more or less known. Or imagine a politically conservative legislature that picks high rates for what it sees as "politically correct" items—solar batteries or organic produce—or a legislature that does not attach penalties to building permits but enacts high taxes on home-construction materials.)

It is absolutely critical to note that one of the many reasons a municipality might well choose a selective sales tax is that the tax could be imposed on those items for which demand was relatively price inelastic, thus insuring that the tax would have limited impact on economic behavior. The ideal tax, in terms of minimizing deadweight loss, would simply be a worldwide head tax (levied on simply existing) since no one could avoid the tax by either changing behavior (from the ideal no-tax-world behavior to some less desirable tax-evading alternative) or moving out of the taxing jurisdiction to avoid the tax. (Assuming, of course, that dying is a not a desirable tax-evading strategy for a significant number of people subject to the tax.) Some taxes may approximate head taxes better than others: if one is levying a sales tax, it is preferable to levy it on goods for which demand is inelastic so that taxpayers do not substitute less desirable goods for ones they would desire more in a no-tax world, as they would if higher-elasticity goods were taxed.[38] The constitutional complaint against such a tax is not clear: the fact that people are taxed equally when they are equal along the dimension of consuming goods for which demand is generally inelastic would seem to be enough to sustain the tax, even though such people might have different incomes, have different aggregate amounts of consumption, or own different amounts of property. It is also of no moment that the generalization that the tax will not alter behavior is imperfect; the

---

38. Municipalities might also use selective sales taxes on the supposition that, for administrative or political reasons, they want to use only sales taxes but want to blunt the regressivity of ordinary sales taxes by exempting items more typically purchased by poorer taxpayers. In particular cases, though, parties with atypical spending patterns will be rewarded or punished by the exemption and will not pay the same tax as similarly situated others pay when they follow the dimensions the legislature thought most relevant. A poor citizen who happened to purchase numerous nonexempt items pays a higher tax than someone similarly situated in terms of both income and aggregate consumption.

fact that, at a minimum, the legislature will sometimes be wrong and will have levied a tax that will alter some consumer conduct surely does not invalidate the tax, and a prudent Court would not invalidate a tax on its own supposition that the legislature picked the wrong items to tax and had thus failed to meet its goals.

Exactions may well, on their face, be taxes that are most perfectly designed to have little impact on behavior. Because they are essentially negotiated with the taxpayer, the municipality can choose to moderate the burden if it believes the taxpayer will either flee the jurisdiction rather than pay the tax or back off development plans in a fashion that the locality finds undesirable. The owner facing an exaction is in the odd position of claiming that the tax is less acceptable than a selective sales tax because it is administratively more precise. Those enacting selective sales taxes may only guess that they are taxing items for which demand is generally price insensitive, while those administering exactions may levy the tax knowing that if they set an overly high rate, the entity will simply withdraw its request for the permit.[39]

Imagine an income tax administrator who knew each class of workers' labor-supply curve and set a very high marginal tax whenever the administrator believed a class of workers earned economic rent. The most difficult point, to which I soon return, is whether it would be constitutionally permissible to base a tax on knowledge of the labor-supply curves of particular people. Thus, could Ken Griffey Jr.'s baseball earnings be taxed at a higher rate than what are assumed, counterfactually, to be equal baseball earnings by Deion Sanders because Sanders has the option of playing football full time so that a high tax on his earnings might have an atypical impact on the allocation of his labor time? Could this unequal taxation be maintained if rather than being directed to undertax Sanders, a named person, or to overtax a larger group of named players, the IRS were directed to give more general sorts of exemptions to people who have earned a certain amount of money outside their primary earning field? Even if this category was known to apply to very few people, all of whose identities could be ascertained by focusing on the question? Is it enough

---

39. As a matter of prudence, the local administrator ought not simply consider whether this particular entity can be taxed without changing its behavior, for example, because it has already sunk costs into the venture that will be unrecoverable if abandoned. A sustainable optimal-tax scheme should not only not change this entity's actions but also signal to new builders that they will pay at least marginally less than the amount that makes them indifferent between engaging in the sort of development the municipality desires and some alternative development path.

that the reason for singling out a taxpayer is a general, public-policy reason rather than capriciousness or arbitrariness?[40]

The point is not whether such a tax is administrable or even unambiguously desirable in efficiency terms given its administrative difficulties.[41] The point is that such a tax is plainly constitutional even though it affects unequally people with the same income.[42]

It appears fairly obvious to me that the interventionist strategy will flounder to the degree that it depends on establishing some list of constitutionally acceptable explicit tax bases.[43] The alternative, of course, is to say that a base is acceptable as long as one can articulate some general rule of taxation, applicable to a substantial number of parties. If this is the test,

40. Imagine, for example, that the tax-administering authority is fairly certain that virtually all professional athletes earn a considerable amount of economic rent. That is to say, the tax-collecting authority believes that when a player earns seven million dollars a year before taxes, his next-best alternatives to playing the sport for one million dollars after taxes—leisure or a job outside the sport—would rarely, if ever, be superior to the one million dollars. It is possible to be rather sure of this supposition because prior to the advent of free agency and the player-salary explosion, there was no evidence that players abandoned the game.

41. It is far easier to determine that those who have already trained as baseball players could be taxed very heavily without altering allocation—whether or not they play baseball—than it is to figure out prospectively what salaries draw people into training for the profession. Moreover, it is possible to believe that it is desirable to allocate players among teams using salary signals, just as some rent-control opponents believe it might be desirable to allocate a fixed number of units among tenants using dollar bids. (I strongly suspect that most sports fans, like rent-control proponents, would argue that such an allocative system has proven quite detrimental.)

42. The tax is constitutional not only because courts are reluctant to second-guess legislative policy judgments even when the courts suspect the legislation could not be justified rationally. Such a tax may well be more economically efficient than a tax that treated taxpayers as relevantly identical if and only if their incomes were the same. Moreover, under certain plausible conceptions of fairness, the tax is fairer as well. Assume that two people have both been making fifty thousand dollars per year, and each gets a raise to seventy-five thousand dollars. Assume further that the raise only marginally compensates one person for the added disutility of taking on more burdensome or annoying work, while for the other, it represents pure economic rent. Those who believe that for fairness reasons both people should each be taxed in relationship to hedonic utility (for which income is just a second-rate approximation) will note that the first person is barely better off now than when she was making only fifty thousand dollars, while life has improved substantially for the second person. For far fuller discussions of issues of taxing surplus, see Fried, "Fairness," 982–85, 1008–1015.

43. Though it is purely speculation, I would guess that one of the reasons that the Court has backed off the more interventionist interpretations of cases like *Nollan* is that at least some members of the Court foresaw that the justices would ultimately be asked to rule on the permissibility of distinct tax bases and would inevitably have to do so without any grounding. As Justice Thomas noted in his *Nordlinger* concurrence, pressing the Court to overrule *Allegheny Pittsburgh Coal:* "The Equal Protection Clause does not prescribe a single method of taxation" (505 U.S. 1, 22).

though, a tax on all landlords to support low-income tenants will surely pass muster, as most likely would a tax on the reasonably large, unnamed group of landlords that has hardship tenants. How exactions (or an income tax keyed to knowledge of particular labor-supply curves) would fare under such a test is less clear. One could argue that both are unduly person specific in the sense that parties could not know their tax liability by looking at general regulations making reference to impersonally known observables.

There are both administrative and theoretical problems with this alternative formulation, however. Administratively, one must ask how a court should recognize when a statute is inadequately general? If all those who seek to expand near the creek in Tigard must add to the easement, is the tax general enough? In this regard, to what degree may the legislature rely on the fact that some taxpayers may pass along a tax to consumers to argue that what appears to be a narrow tax is in fact reasonably broadly based? If all those who seek to expand near the creek must pay the tax unless they get a variance (the regulatory equivalent of a property tax abatement or exemption), is that condition general enough, even though those who receive variances may arguably be members of the same class?

More interestingly, it is not clear whether a tax is adequately general if a broadly dispersed group of citizens is subject to some liability, but the precise level of liability varies on a case-by-case basis without regard to general rules. Thus, does the statement in the ADA that every public-accommodation owner owes disabled customers reasonable accommodation state an implicit tax liability that is general enough, or does the fact that the dollar amount of the liability will turn on particular facts about the owner's business and the nature of the required accommodation make such a regulatory tax suspect? Is it sufficient that some tax applies to all public-accommodation owners (or even to all those opening new public accommodations)? If so, there appears to be nothing problematic in either *Nollan* or *Dolan,* since what is, for argument's sake, a tax to be used for general public purposes rather than a substitute for regulation or a user fee applies to all coastal owners who seek to develop. Or is the tax insufficient because its size is facially indeterminate?

The fact that parties may often bear distinct financial obligations when asked to comply with nominally equal obligations poses a more sweeping embarrassment for Scalia's general theory. Everyone is governed by the same nominal common law of nuisance, which forbids, for example, undertaking activities that impose substantial (or, in other jurisdictions, substantial non-cost-justified) losses on neighboring property owners. But the precise content of this obligation—the distinct costs each person bears—is as dependent on the identity of particular neighbors as the San Jose landlords' obligation to lower costs in *Pennell* is dependent on the tenants' identity. Some people may be entitled to make a certain amount of noise; others must change their conduct or abate that same amount of noise, depending on the particular activities in which others have chosen to engage.

One might say, to track my earlier account of Scalia's scheme, that the concept of exploitation is (at least permissibly) victim-specific: what counts as an exploitative price depends on the identity of the buyer. Such could surely be the case in relationship to an expansive law of duress of fraud/information-sharing. Everyone may all be bound to protect those with whom they deal against certain sorts of improvident decisions, yet the costs of complying with this general mandate for sellers who deal with customers with greater levels of cognitive impairments, impulsiveness, or lack of information may be substantially higher than the costs borne by those who deal with more self-protective buyers. Nonetheless, the expansive, consumer-specific law of consumer protection should still be reviewed deferentially.

Thus, the line between the traditional regulatory functions and traditional redistributive functions is simply less sharp than one must imagine to make Scalia's scheme workable. Alternatively, it is possible to simply believe that the fact that traditional common law regulation poses few problems, though it imposes distinct taxlike burdens on parties, ought to make people less wary of the fact that either explicit taxes or new regulation may also impose uneven burdens.

The second major problem is theoretical: What might ultimately be gained, substantively, from invalidating an unduly narrow tax? I will return to that point only after considering a closely related issue: Should the court intervene to invalidate an unduly broad tax?

(iii) Should One Care about Unduly Broad Taxes?

From a libertarian viewpoint, it is just as troublesome to collect a general tax to pay for something for which a private individual or individuals should pay as it is to make private individuals shoulder the costs of public programs. Take the *Dolan* case. Assume, at least for argument's sake, that particular landowners living proximate to the creek gain a great deal more from flood protection than do citizens of Tigard living further away from the creek. Should the general taxpayers not have a just complaint that they have had property expropriated if the government substitutes a tax-and-spend program either for a benefits tax/user fee (charging floodplain occupants the bulk of the price of whatever flood-risk-reducing public improvements are built) or for inaction (letting private parties bear or avert the losses from flooding themselves)? Libertarian theory is rights-protective: the fact that a majority of the town rather than a minority is stripped of its rights by a general tax is of no moment. Individuals who are coerced into transferring funds for projects that are not truly public or to pay for problems they did not cause should get no comfort (from a libertarian perspective) from the fact that the tax was voluntarily accepted by similarly situated neighbors who in some ways resemble the people coerced, just as the Dolans are not thought to be adequately protected by simple democracy.

Many would argue that the failure of the sorts of interventionists I describe in this chapter to favor judicially mandated user charges or inaction simply demonstrates that they are not libertarians, a point that was already dramatically obvious given their deference to taxation more generally and to legislative determinations that regulations avert unwarranted social costs or unjust exploitation of contractual partners. If this interventionist program is not libertarian, however, what is it? One answer is that it focuses on political-process concerns. In this view, the interventionists are undisturbed when the public at large pays for private benefits because the taxpayers of Tigard can adequately protect themselves: they have imposed a tax on themselves and need no constitutional protection from democracy.[44]

---

44. This is another variant on Ely's argument recommending court deference to affirmative action, on the ground that the white majority group that disadvantages itself by enacting preferences for African Americans is not politically isolated or powerless. See John Hart Ely, *Democracy and Distrust* (Cambridge: Harvard University Press, 1980), 170–72. The responses to the argument in the text and the Ely arguments on affirmative action are, of course, structurally the same. Some who oppose affirmative action will assert (rather mysteriously in my view) that the "right" to (what they see as) meritocratic treatment is not up for democratic grabs. Opponents of affirmative action willing to engage the political-process point more directly will typically note that the groupings are arbitrary. The fact that someone who loses out as a result of what he sees as an unjust race-based preference program is a member of a majority group (whites) that generally has reasonable political access and bargaining power does not really mean that he is a member of more relevantly empowered political groups or that his voice was heard or his capacity to horse-trade uncompromised. Some of Tigard's townspeople who taxed themselves to protect creek-abutting flood victims may have gotten something back from the downtown businessmen; some may rightly feel like they gave yet got nothing.

The point seems quite troublesome. First, it seems to ignore the very real possibility that majorities can readily single out and harm minorities without using narrow taxes as long as it is understood that the choice between user fees (or inaction) and taxing and spending cannot be scrutinized. A governmental entity may charge justified user fees for only a small subset of the services for which benefits are concentrated. The user fee itself will be free from scrutiny (since it is facially legitimate), while the decision not to charge user fees for services for more politically potent constituencies (whether bare majorities or empowered minorities) is likewise left unexamined. Imagine, for example, a quite plausible scenario in which the local governmental entity charges user fees for the marina and the golf course but not for equally privately beneficial playgrounds and baseball fields (as well as the town dump, bike path maintenance, and schools), knowing full well the rough identities and traits of those who will both bear the selectively imposed user fees and pay taxes that subsidize the services utilized exclusively by the majority, which could have been subject to user fees.[45]

Second, this position seems unduly oblivious to the argument that majorities may readily be victimized by organized minorities.[46] The idea that the political process is unproblematic whenever legislatures vote is hardly unassailable.

It may be reasonable to be suspicious of all governmental programs in which parties decide issues knowing how that decision will affect known people. The Rawlsian veil of ignorance does indeed promote civic-mindedness and a search for just rather than self-serving legislation. Majorities

---

45. Or, to track the example I used in talking about selective sales taxes, imagine a politically conservative town that charges user fees for alternative energy projects but subsidizes conventional power or a state that supports state research on conventional but not organic agricultural innovation. It may be the case that a jurisdiction could, under the more expansive understandings of unconstitutional conditions analysis that Sullivan has expounded, run into some problems if its selective subsidy pattern compromised or pressured the exercise of constitutional rights (e.g., imagine subsidizing childbirth but not abortion, though the state could not directly manifest its disapproval of abortion; imagine viewpoint-dependent subsidies). See Sullivan, "Unconstitutional Conditions," 1489–1504. But even an expansive reading of this doctrine will cover few cases in which majorities or politically powerful minorities simply insure a more favorable post-state-action distribution for themselves.

46. See, e.g., Sam Peltzman, "Toward a More General Theory of Regulation," *J. of L. and Econ.* 19 (1976): 211; Gary Becker, "A Theory of Competition among Pressure Groups for Political Influence," *Q. J. of Econ.* 98 (1983): 371; George Stigler, "The Theory of Economic Regulation," *Bell J. of Econ. and Mgmt. Sci.* 2 (1971): 3. I believe this argument is often stated with undue certainty; such public-choice accounts of legislation are, in my view, frequently wrong, though they may be more or less correct in particular cases. See Mark Kelman, "On Democracy-Bashing," 199.

may well be especially tempted to gather benefits for themselves while imposing costs on the minority (just as well-organized minorities will be tempted to stick it to the widely dispersed and difficult-to-organize public). But the Court cannot really invalidate every statute in which a legislature knowingly gouged the economic interests of a political out-group. As the Court notes, quite reasonably, in *Nordlinger,* the manifest injustices of Proposition 13 may well go uncorrected by the political process: "Certainly," Justice Blackmun writes, "California's grand experiment appears to vest benefits in a broad, powerful, and entrenched segment of society . . . and ordinary democratic processes may be unlikely to prompt its reconsideration."[47]

## (iv) So, What Is Important?

In invalidating an unduly narrow regulatory tax, interventionists could not, it seems, really be seeking improvements in the political process. Legislation is generally both more opaque (as to the actual distributive impact of either tax or spending programs) and more transparent (as to the intended beneficiaries and losers of each sort of program) than those who believe regulation must be specially scrutinized imply. Such invalidations also do not protect any individual's substantive entitlement to a certain level of posttax, posttransfer income. Taxpayers generally may be asked to finance programs of special benefit to individuals or narrow subgroups, which erodes libertarian entitlements just as much as when an individual is asked to fund programs of general benefit.

What should interventionists seek, then? I think, at most, they can hope only to prohibit imposing atypically high tax burdens on parties that are identified or identifiable as individuals. The goal is very limited. Even tax legislation that is personal on its face is all right provided it singles out people to pay atypically low rates rather than atypically high ones.

It is hard to imagine why a court would interfere with the authority of local governments to grant local property tax abatements to any particular named party, given the importance of such abatements in fostering local development.[48] Thus, a local property tax abatement system would become

---

47. *Nordlinger v. Hahn,* 18.

48. For examples of local property tax abatements designed to encourage particular entities to stay or to locate in a particular jurisdiction, see, e.g., Andrew L. Kolesar, "Can State and Local Tax Incentives and Other Contributions Stimulate Economic Development," *Tax Law* 44 (1990): 285, 287–88 (GM's Saturn plant lured to Spring Hill, Tennessee, in 1985 by an economic-incentive package that included seventy million dollars in local property tax

impermissible only as abatements were granted more and more routinely so that the very occasional nonexempt party were personally identifiable.

Federal income tax rules can even exempt or favor single parties, though the convention is not to name the party but to apply the favor to a class of parties that happens to have but one member. Most highly particularistic federal tax legislation is found in transition rules, exempting certain taxpayers from the impact of tax law changes. These rules do not appear in the code itself but are footnotes or endnotes to newly enacted sections.[49] Again, while such exemptions may in fact frequently result from corrupt influence peddling, the possibility that the exemption serves to meet allocative or fairness goals should preclude real judicial scrutiny.

In the final analysis, then, there is less protection against biased distribution of burdens (which can just as readily occur when small groups are victimized by overly high taxes or spending programs that exclude these groups) than against the breach of impersonality. The fear is the intrusive Orwellian tax collector, with undue knowledge about and concern over features of one's private situation that permit a too precise assessment of how the taxpayer might respond to government intrusion.[50]

---

abatements); Alex Kotlowitz and Dale D. Buss, "Costly Bait: Localities' Giveaways to Lure Corporations Cause Growing Outcry," *Wall Street Journal,* Sep. 24, 1986, 27 (Ohio promises Honda Motor Co. fifteen years of property tax abatements on an auto and motorcycle complex built in 1977); Joseph William Singer, "The Reliance Interest in Property," *Stanford L. Rev.* 40 (1988): 611, 615 n. 15 (between 1980 and 1984, Chicago granted U.S. Steel local property tax abatements worth tens of millions of dollars to induce the company to keep its South Works steel plant open).

49. Thus, for example, certain readily identified entities were exempted from the application of the repeal of §336 of the code in the Tax Reform Act of 1986 (which had allowed tax-free distributions of appreciated property in complete corporate liquidations). See, e.g., §633(e) of PL 99-514 (100 STAT. 2280), which provided, in part, "The amendments made by this subtitle shall not apply to any liquidation of a corporation formed under the laws of Pennsylvania on August 3, 1970 if . . . an agreement for the sale of a material portion of the assets of such corporation was signed on May 9, 1986" and went on to specify three other identifiable entities exempted from the more stringent tax treatment.

Particularistic tax legislation is more frequently directed not at individuals or individual entities but industries: For example, §613 and §613A of the code contain percentage depletion allowance rules that favor the covered industries listed in §§613(b) and 613A(b); these listed industries may depreciate/amortize a sum larger than the cost of their initial investment; moreover, even among these favored extractive industries, some are favored by extremely rapid (22 percent) cost-recapture provisions, while others may deduct as little as 5 percent per annum.

50. The opposition to such tax "bills of attainder" may derive as well from the belief that taxpayers are entitled to retain some of the economic rents they earn—i.e., that taxpayers want to restrain the government's ability to seize surplus. Such opposition might also be motivated by the belief that it will help guard against both arbitrariness and discrimination, on the supposition that direct prohibitions of such arbitrariness or discrimination may be difficult for courts to enforce fully.

In an odd way, regulatory takings law should become a minor offshoot of privacy law, driven more by the (traditionally politically progressive) anti-statist sentiments associated with zealous Fourth Amendment advocacy than the (typically right-wing) antistatist sentiments associated with the property-rights-protection movement.

# CHAPTER 4

# Prudential Concerns (I):
# Public Finance Considerations

### The Analytical Framework:
### A First Statement of the Argument

Traditional regulatory commands impose direct costs on the regulated parties, which they might or might not ultimately bear, while compliance with these commands distributes benefits more or less broadly. Similarly, traditional taxes impose costs either on those who directly pay the relevant tax or on some other parties, depending on the incidence of the tax, while the funds raised through taxation are expended in a fashion that distributes benefits to broad or narrow groups. User fees do not impose net costs on any service user. Users may gain surplus, valuing the service more than the price of receiving it, but they will not pay more than the service is worth to them. (This phenomenon will hold true, at least tautologically, if one has a choice about whether to bear user fees. If, instead, the governmental entity charges compulsory fees or imposes benefit taxes on those citizens it believes particularly benefit from a program, as the government will typically do when it is difficult to exclude some beneficiaries from enjoying the benefits of services whether or not the beneficiaries pay for the services, it is of course possible that some people will be charged more than they gain from the program.) Third parties, again a narrow or broad range, who contribute nothing to financing a particular program may nonetheless receive some of the benefits from a program fully funded by user fees. (For example, one could imagine charging national park users entrance fees that covered costs of maintaining and preserving the parks. Users would, tautologically, bear no net costs since benefits would be at least equal to fees to the prospective users, or they would forbear from use. But some nonusers might benefit as well, for example, because the value of their implicit option to visit the park site would be increased if user fees served to preserve the park.) Government inaction permits defined citizen groups to bear certain costs; one might correlatively describe those who are relieved from the obligation to pay taxes that would fund a more interventionist alternative as benefiting from inaction if the baseline were such that would-be taxpayers expected to bear higher taxes.

Whenever the regulatory option is employed, the first consideration ought therefore to be whether costs have been imposed on parties in a sensible way, compared to the alternative distributions of costs. In a sense, all that is asked is which form of levy is most desirable; alternative taxes are simply compared in terms of fairness, administrative efficiency, and allocative effects.[1] My sense is that opponents of regulatory taxation have typically slighted the possible advantages of regulatory taxes, particularly along the allocative dimension. In some cases, regulations may be a more allocatively neutral means to raise revenues than broad-based taxes.

Kaplow and Shavell note, quite correctly, that the income tax dominates, in efficiency terms, any regulation (or private law rule) imposed on a party to redistribute, levied by virtue of wealth or income, given certain restrictive assumptions.[2] Thus, to take the simplest case, if, to redistribute income, richer defendants in tort cases are made to pay higher damages than poorer ones, the higher damage judgments will, in effect, increase the marginal income tax rate on a probabilistic basis for those who would be harmed by this practice. The practice will thus have all the disincentive effects of an explicit increase in marginal rates plus the allocative problems inherent in overdeterring harm-causing activity by overstating damages.

The point is correct, in terms of actual incentive effects, only if one assumes—quite unrealistically—that as a behavioral matter, people will assess their taxes on a rational expected-tax basis, treating taxes that are certain to be levied on income and low-probability damage judgments that will be levied on income if they happen to be found liable in precisely the same way. It is likely, though, that rational agents with ordinary information-processing limits who are considering whether to take higher paying but more annoying jobs will measure the increase in wages net of the taxes the agents are certain to pay given published income tax rates; hence, they

---

1. Thus, one should attempt to ascertain whether people have been justly selected to bear the costs, whether the costs are imposed in an administratively efficacious way, and whether the imposition of costs through this mechanism is more or less likely to alter the behavior of parties who will have to bear the costs in an undesirable way.

2. See Steven Shavell and Louis Kaplow, "Why the Legal System Is Less Efficient Than the Income Tax in Redistributing Income," *J. of Legal Studies* 23 (1994): 667.

face income tax-based disincentives to move to the more productive setting. Whether the rational agents will also measure raises net of the expected increase in damage judgments that they will face if they become richer on the off-chance that they happen to be defendants in tort suits is not at all obvious. Attention to distribution in tort suits might therefore function as a perennially unanticipated ex post tax with few allocative effects. Nonetheless, the point remains valid on the odd assumption that agents have perfect foresight and perfectly process information about low-probability events.

It is important to note as well that Shavell and Kaplow are criticizing only those regulations (or private law rules) that are themselves allocatively inefficient and (to foreshadow a point to which I return in more detail) that predictably bear more heavily on actors when income increases. Regulations (and private law rules) might meet classic redistributive egalitarian ends but be (at least equally) motivated by their favorable or neutral impact on behavior. Monopolists' price regulations, for example, might typically redistribute from richer to poorer citizens but also decrease the untoward allocative effects of (non-price-discriminating) monopolistic pricing. An income tax used to fund low-income housing programs will have some adverse allocative impact on work and savings decisions; an ideal rent-control statute, eliminating only the capacity of landlords to charge scarcity rents on already-existing units, has few adverse allocative effects on the taxpayer side, though it arguably misallocates among buyers, assuming one wants to ration the scarce good by willingness to pay.

Moreover, though regulations may often seem unfair in horizontal equity terms, it is far from clear that broad-based tax-and-spend programs should invariably seem any less unfair, in part because broad-based tax programs are imperfectly administered. More subtly, though, a broad-based tax-and-spend program may allow those who are in fact particularly responsible for social problems to spread the costs of solving them to others not responsible for the problems or permit concentrated beneficiaries of certain programs to evade the responsibility to pay explicit or implicit user fees/benefit taxes. Similarly, such broad-based programs may allow parties who ought to bear costs privately, because the state should remain inactive, to force others to share losses.

At the same time, it is important to consider the relative efficacy of providing benefits to a target population by regulating private action rather than direct action by the state. If, for example, the regulated party must provide a service, would it do so more or less effectively than the state itself?[3] Even in cases in which it is clear that the private party would better provide the relevant benefit, the question remains whether the private party would better provide the benefit if uncompensated than if compensated.[4] There may well be situations in which private parties will misdesign service programs if the government fully compensates them for all their expenditures. It is not obvious, for example, that if the state agrees to defray the costs to store owners who retrofit their buildings, it will be able effectively to monitor the level of expenditures for reasonableness and/or fraud. Moral-hazard and other problems may often render compensation undesirable.

There are also political-process issues inevitably lurking in the choice among these goal-meeting options, which I address in the next chapter. Those interested in improving the functioning of collective decision making have typically emphasized the virtues of systems that make the cost of implicit government programs more transparent and illustrate more clearly who wins and loses each time the government acts. Furthermore, these scholars have argued that regulation is likely to be less transparent than other forms of government action.[5] Furthermore, state bureaucrats

---

3. For example, will store owners do a more or less cost-effective job than a state authority in retrofitting stores to make them accessible to those with mobility impairments? If the regulated party must provide a service at a regulated price, will this aid targeted beneficiaries more or less than would direct government aid in purchasing the good or service at market prices, whether through cash grants or vouchers? For another discussion of this issue, in draft at the same time that I was first presenting these ideas, see Julie A. Roin, "Reconceptualizing Unfunded Mandates and Other Regulations," 93 *NW. U. L. Rev.* 351 (1999).

4. In some situations, it is the only question. Where the regulated party is simply asked to forbear from taking certain steps (e.g., where a local government adopts a restrictive zoning plan; where the state or federal government enacts restrictive conservation regulations), the relevant question is not whether the government will directly supply a superior substitute service (e.g., public parks that somehow make up for the loss of green space that restrictive zoning might otherwise preserve) but whether the benefits of forbearance would be equally available if the state purchased agreements from the relevant private parties to forbear from conduct (e.g., nondevelopment servitudes from otherwise-zoned property owners) or otherwise compensated them for the losses sustained as a result of the restrictive regulations.

5. As Justice Scalia says in the *Pennell* dissent,

Of course all regulation effects wealth transfers. When excessive rents are forbidden . . . landlords as a class become poorer and . . . at least incumbent tenants as a class become richer. Singling out landlords to be the transferors may be within our traditional constitutional notions of fairness, because they can plausibly be viewed as the source or the beneficiary of the high-rent problem. Once such a connection is no longer required, however, there is no end to the social transformations that can be accomplished by so-called "regulation," at great expense to the democratic process.

facing constrained money-denominated budgets will allocate resources improperly if they can obtain certain goals off budget. Less cost-effective programs might be chosen over more cost-effective ones in which actual dollars must be spent.[6] I question these assumptions but argue that there may be some distinct process problems inherent in using regulation.

## The Burden Side

I have emphasized throughout this book that a government may confront what it perceives to be a social problem in four main ways, each of which imposes costs on different groups. The state entity may simply decide to do nothing and let private actors bear losses it might otherwise choose to avert.[7] It may decide to run a program (directly or by contracting service provision out to a private operating entity) but charge users directly, particularly if would-be users could be readily excluded from receiving the relevant service, or through a benefits tax if users could not be readily excluded.[8] The state may regulate conduct that is otherwise problematic to

> The politically attractive feature of regulation is not that it permits wealth transfers to be achieved that could not be achieved otherwise; but rather that it permits them to be achieved "off-budget," with relative invisibility and thus relative immunity from normal democratic processes. . . . Subsidies for . . . groups may well be a good idea, but because of the operation of the Takings Clause our governmental system has required them to be applied, in general, through the system of taxing and spending, where both economic effects and competing priorities are more evident." (*Pennell v. City of San Jose,* 22–23)

Others argue that regulation is bad in process terms because it is all too transparent that it can be used by the majority to impose all the costs of a program on subgroups of the population. This phenomenon causes majorities to misassess whether benefits are worth their cost (since they do not privately bear these costs in any case) and to focus their political attention less on the public good than on their more particular aims.

6. See, e.g., Posner, *Economic Analysis,* 58–59.

7. Here are some examples of inaction strategies: Cities need not enact zoning plans; parties that would have benefited if their neighbors were more restricted in how they could use property would then suffer losses (and would suffer still more losses if the state narrowed its nuisance law), either because they had to expend funds to purchase negative equitable servitudes or because the value of their property would fall. The federal government need not maintain the National Park Service, funded through taxes; it could auction off existing parkland to private developers, who could choose to charge entrance fees or to sell the land off to mining interests if that proved more profitable. Would-be park users (as well as those with political commitments to naturalism and those with a desire to maintain use options for themselves or their descendants) would bear costs they do not now shoulder.

8. The federal government could maintain national parks but charge those who visit the parks an unsubsidized price; it could do so whether it operated the parks or contracted out operations to a private entity that was contractually obliged to operate the land as a park.

avert the problem.[9] The government may establish a wide variety of taxes to fund perceived needs—taxes on income, consumption, consumption of certain items,[10] real property, personal property, imports (tariffs), excess profits,[11] profits earned by some or all sorts of corporate entities, gifts, or

---

The federal government could build dams to increase water supplies but charge water users unsubsidized prices. Cities could collect taxes earmarked for fire protection based on the projected costs of fire fighting: high-rise owners might pay more, as might those with less fireproof buildings. Air-quality control projects, whose users are not readily excluded, might be funded by some combination of benefit taxes (set highest for those residing in areas in which air quality is otherwise most problematic, e.g., because the area is located in a basin that typically traps pollutants) and implicit nuisance fees (surcharges for activities that most compromise air quality).

9. Municipalities may enact zoning plans; the federal government may mandate that habitats necessary to preserve the viability of certain species be maintained by those who own the sensitive habitats; emissions from cars and power plants may be limited; fire-fighting costs may be limited by enacting a building code that mandates more and better sprinklers or fire-retardant materials.

10. There might be fairly broad-based sales taxes with relatively few or no exemptions or sales taxes levied on a rather narrow list of items (usually luxury taxes). A sales tax, whether broadly or narrowly based, might be direct (as most state and municipal sales taxes are now, as VATs would be if enacted) or implicit (as is the denial of an otherwise-available deduction for certain items in the federal income tax). Thus, one could think of the denial in §280F of the Internal Revenue Code of full deductions for otherwise-deductible luxury cars as a form of federal luxury sales tax on those items. Naturally, there is some question about whether the deduction restriction acts as an implicit tax or better implements a more ideal income tax. Some would argue that in cases in which taxpayers embed unneeded consumption benefits in their business expenditures by purchasing products of which only some more austere version is actually necessary to generate income, net taxable income is best measured net only of that portion of the spending needed to generate the income.

This dilemma simply states the common problem in distinguishing tax expenditures (deliberate forbearance from the collection of taxes, designed to encourage particular activity and often replacing explicit programs for spending on the same activity) from appropriate deductions: Do deductions for health care expenditures (or noninclusion of health insurance benefits in income) act as an implicit government-funded health care program, or do they realize the goal of measuring income properly by excluding from income funds expended to return taxpayers to some premorbidity baseline of good health? For general discussions of the ambiguity of the tax-expenditure concept, see, e.g., Boris Bittker, "Accounting for Federal 'Tax Subsidies' in the National Budget," *Nat. Tax. J.* 22 (1969): 244; Boris Bittker, "The Tax Expenditure Budget—A Reply to Professors Surrey and Hellmuth," *Nat. Tax. J.* 22 (1969): 538. For discussions of the issue in relationship to health care, compare William Andrews, "Personal Deductions in an Ideal Income Tax," *Harvard L. Rev.* 86 (1972): 309 (medical care deduction is needed to measure income properly), with Mark Kelman, "Personal Deductions Revisited: Why They Fit Poorly in an 'Ideal' Income Tax and Why They Fit Worse in a Far from Ideal World," *Stanford L. Rev.* 31 (1979): 831, 858–79 (availability of the medical care deduction misstates taxpayers' relative incomes).

11. Some taxes are clearly directed at excess profits (or economic rents)—e.g., the federal government levied a tax on excess profits in the oil industry in the mid-1970s, when worldwide crude prices rose dramatically in part as a result of OPEC's success in restricting production. It is possible, of course, to view existing progressive rate structures in routine income

bequests. In each case, it is vital to consider first whether the parties who will bear costs will change behavior in a desirable or undesirable way to avoid bearing costs. It is also necessary to consider whether it is unduly administratively costly to impose costs on private parties in the chosen fashion and, finally, whether the choice of parties to bear costs comports with fairness norms.

## 1.   What Will the Parties Do to Avoid Bearing the Costs?

There is no categorical response to each form of policy instrument that permits evaluation of the efficacy of these policies in some general sense. Thus, for example, the behavioral response to the imposition of sales taxes is not always the same but will typically depend on more particular empirical facts, most notably the sales tax level and the demand elasticity for the taxed good. Nonetheless, it is helpful to think about citizens' prototypical behavioral responses to each sort of government program.

### (a) Government inaction

Broadly speaking, private actors can evade the costs of government inaction only by either altering their behavior so that these costs are reduced or by insuring against loss. At times, of course, each citizen will internalize all or nearly all the costs of government inaction. (Imagine a fire department's refusal to tend to fires in remote areas unless risks to other property owners were substantial.) At other times, the citizen might have some private incentive to reduce a problem about which the government was passive but would still not bear all relevant social costs. (Imagine the municipality refusing to dispose of garbage. Particular property owners will bear some but not all costs if they continue to generate substantial levels of garbage that are not disposed of, but neighbors will bear some costs as well.)[12]

---

tax systems as a method for imposing an administratively imperfect tax on economic rents: in this view, higher earners typically earn returns in excess of those needed to induce the earners to supply the specialized labor they would provide at lower net wage rates, so that (relatively) high marginal tax rates simply transfer some of those rents to public users. See Barbara Fried, *The Progressive Assault on Laissez Faire: Robert Hale and the First Law and Economics Movement* (Cambridge: Harvard University Press, 1998), 149–59 (detailing the history of this idea among progressive economists).

12. There are certainly times when it appears that the incentives for the private party to reduce the problem are sufficiently powerful for it to take socially optimal steps, even though a social surplus is generated when it does so. Thus, private owners might be trusted to select optimal strategies to deal with rodent infestation, even though others will benefit if they get rid of the rodents; this decision depends on whether there is incremental value to taking certain precautionary expenditures that might be irrational for owners themselves to take.

Generally speaking, the government will adopt an inaction strategy because it feels that allowing private parties to bear certain costs will induce them to take the desirable (from a social perspective) step of avoiding the costs because private parties are the cheapest cost-avoiders.[13]

However, the fact that an explicit government program may increase social losses compared to an inaction strategy (e.g., through creating moral-hazard problems) does not mean that such is the case. There will be nothing resembling strong empirical consensus in trying to identify situations in which moral-hazard problems are most pronounced. For example, Federal Emergency Management Agency relief programs may or may not unduly encourage parties to overbuild in areas atypically subject to natural disaster.[14] Similarly, some would argue that if the problem is to reduce the ill consequences of unemployment, the best strategy is inaction, since only then will workers face appropriate incentives to shorten or avoid spells of unemployment. However, as an empirical matter, unemployment insurance may or may not in fact substantially increase the incidence and duration of unemployment.[15] Moreover, the optimal duration of job search is not obvious. Thus, it is necessary to know not only the behavioral impact of a move from the tax-and-spend program to inaction but also how the shift should be evaluated. In some sense, one would think that the norm here might be relatively clear: a party should continue to search only when

13. In this sense, it might be more apt, conceptually, to argue that the virtues of the inaction strategy are virtues not on the implicit tax side but on the implicit spending side. Those who are burdened by government inaction also benefit from the steps that are taken—by the burdened parties themselves—to minimize the social problem that is deliberately left to be dealt with privately rather than solved through some more explicit collective program. The arguments in favor of inaction are typically that private parties will do a better job solving the problem in a less costly fashion or that, distributively, no one else ought to bear the relevant costs. One can describe this argument, then, as saying either that there will be favorable rather than perverse responses to the tax or that the spending party will be more effective than a government provider or regulator.

14. A typical, nonempirical argument asserting that such programs will have this untoward effect is found in Saul Levmore, "Coalitions and Quakes: Disaster Relief and Its Prevention," *U. of Chicago L. School Roundtable* 3 (1996): 1, 7–8.

15. Compare, e.g., Martin Feldstein, "Temporary Layoffs in the Theory of Unemployment," *J. of Pol. Econ.* 84 (1976): 917, and Robert Moffitt and Walter Nicholson, "The Effect of Unemployment Insurance on Unemployment: The Case of Federal Supplemental Benefits," *Rev. of Econ. and Stat.* 63 (1982): 1 (both arguing that unemployment insurance has substantial effects on unemployment and unemployment duration), with Daniel S. Hammermesh, *Jobless Pay and the Economy* (Baltimore: Johns Hopkins University Press, 1977), 32–39, and Stephen T. Marston, "The Impact of Unemployment on Job Search," *Brookings Papers on Econ. Activity* 13 (1975) (offering low estimates of impact of unemployment insurance).

the expected prospective increase in discounted lifetime income (broadly defined so that all improvements in, for example, job satisfaction are monetized) that increased search would generate are greater than the losses from not working. If unemployed workers are spared (some substantial portion of the) losses as a result of government-provided insurance, they will oversearch. But in the absence of perfect capital markets, which would permit them to borrow readily against the higher future earnings increased search might bring, it is not clear that unemployed workers will not accept new job offers prematurely as a result of liquidity constraints unless the state insures them against wage loss.[16]

Even if a program causes social losses to rise, it does not automatically permit the conclusion that the program reduces social welfare. It might be desirable to redistribute a lower net social product. Thus, for example, casualty insurance may at least marginally increase casualties and hence social costs but still increase social welfare because the insurance better distributes losses, given both loss aversion and the declining marginal utility of income.

---

16. Similarly, the provision of public welfare (e.g., AFDC or food stamps) may or may not increase birthrates or dependency relative to the inaction (no welfare) strategy. Compare, e.g., Charles Murray, *Losing Ground: American Social Policy 1950–1980* (New York: Basic Books, 1984) (arguing that welfare increased dependency and illegitimate births), with David Ellwood and Laurence Summers, "Poverty in America: Is Welfare the Answer or the Problem?" in *Fighting Poverty: What Works and What Doesn't,* ed. S. Danziger and D. Weinberg (Cambridge: Harvard University Press, 1986) (welfare's muted impact on withdrawal from labor force, long-term dependency, and birthrates).

Even if the effects on, for example, fertility were less ambiguous, it is important to recall, once again, that policymakers must understand their own preferences as well as come to conclusions about the empirical impact of different governmental decisions. If it were assumed, for argument's sake, that the behavioral effect of a cutoff of transfer payments (whether AFDC historically or TANF today) would be to reduce fertility to some extent, it would be necessary to know how to evaluate whether such a reduction was a desirable or undesirable behavioral outcome. One would have to decide whether the ideal fertility rate (for those whose fertility rates would fall) should reflect policymakers' preferences and/or the preferences of the women whose decisions would change if the government substituted inaction for a tax-and-spend program to deal with the problem of poverty. If the latter were the case, one would also have to decide how to judge what these women's ideal preferences are, given that the preferences differ under each sort of background circumstances. Some might argue, for example, that the ideal fertility rate is the rate that mothers themselves desire in a world in which their personal financial circumstances do not change depending on the number of children they have, but this view is hardly uncontroversial: for most parents who receive no explicit public assistance, children are (at least somewhat) costly. See, generally, Christopher Jencks and Kathryn Edin, "Do Poor Women Have a Right to Bear Children?" *American Prospect* 20 (1995): 43 (the sorts of controls that would realistically dampen fertility—e.g., compulsory Norplant implants and forced sterilization—are all politically unacceptable).

Inaction is generally thought to be a poor strategy when coordination problems among private actors prevent the formation of private consortia that would establish appropriately scaled solutions. But there are certainly controversies about the situations in which such coordination problems exist, even when virtually everyone would concede that scattered individual efforts to minimize social costs would be inapt.[17]

### (b) User fees

Private parties can evade voluntary user fees simply by not purchasing the government service. As long as third parties would not significantly benefit if the services were purchased by users, and as long as the public provider is not wary, for paternalistic reasons, of the wisdom of the decision maker's failure to purchase, this response is typically unproblematic. The service is presumptively not worth its cost to people who choose not to avail themselves of the service.

Obviously, though, in many situations in which the government chooses to employ user fees, third parties also gain from the use.[18] If third parties benefit, of course, the actor's decision to forgo the purchase of the government's service may be privately rational but socially undesirable: subsidized provision theoretically dominates in such cases. Administrative difficulties will abound, though, when one tries to determine the appropriate size of the subsidy or weigh the dangers of overconsumption with a subsidy against the risk of underconsumption without one. The degree to which third parties really benefit, for example, from having educated compatriots is open to both empirical and philosophical question.[19]

---

17. The classic example of a good that theorists predict would be undersupplied by private parties is lighthouses, yet some argue that private parties will solve coordination problems even in providing that quintessentially public good. R. H. Coase, for example, argued that shipwrecks would be prevented by fee-for-service privately operated lighthouses ("The Lighthouse in Economics," *J. of L. and Econ.* 17 [1974]: 357, 375).

18. Thus, to reiterate an earlier example, users of national parks who pay to preserve them help maintain them for those with political attachments to their maintenance and those who wish to preserve an option for use by themselves or their descendants; neither of these second two groups is readily identified or, even if identified, charged. Similarly, third parties may benefit from other citizens' decisions to purchase state-provided schooling (or drug and alcohol rehab services or psychological counseling that reduces abusiveness), but it is easiest both to identify and exact a fee from the primary recipient of the service.

19. Some of the philosophical questions about user fees may be quite intractable. The question of whether particular people benefit so atypically from a government program that it is appropriate for them to bear its costs depends on highly contested assumptions about the degree to which individuals within communities are altruistically linked as individuals and/or

## (c) Regulation

Regulatory evasion strategies are complex and must surely be considered on a case-by-case basis. For example, regulations that demand that certain costly benefits be provided to certain employees might induce parties to avoid hiring those potential employees.[20] If it is too costly to provide the property, services, or cash that a government seeks to exact when property is developed, the property owner might choose not to proceed with development. Demands to preserve still-fragile, high-quality natural environments or man-made ones (e.g., historic-preservation ordinances) might induce parties to destroy[21] the sorts of environments regulators want to preserve before they are subject to preservation requirements.[22] Similarly,

---

all subsumed in some broader community. Take the classic public good, defense. Assume that as an empirical fact, individuals living in New York City are more likely to be killed by nuclear attacks than those living in Montana. The question of whether an attack that kills New Yorkers is a nondifferentiable attack on the United States, so that all citizens benefit from averting such an attack, or an attack of most concern to a subset of Americans is not just empirical but complex and normative.

20. Thus, one would expect that regulations forbidding low-cost discharge would have some disemployment effect; that antidiscrimination rules that made it more likely that one would be sued if one discharged protected rather than unprotected employees would have some negative effect on the employment levels of protected workers; that the ADA's requirement to accommodate disabled workers without charging them the costs of accommodation would lead to some disemployment effects on disabled workers; that the requirement that employers pay workers some minimum wage would block the employment of at least some workers who would willingly work for a lower wage. As I note in the text, the direction of these effects is far clearer than their magnitude.

21. One might also argue, as Donald Wittman did, that historic-preservation regulations would, at the margin, induce parties not to create interesting buildings since building a high-quality building might ultimately subject the parcel owner to income-reducing regulation. See Wittman, "Liability for Harm or Restitution for Benefit?" *J. of Legal Stud.* 13 (1984): 57, 74–75. But it seems unlikely, given typical discount rates for low-probability events in the distant future, that the magnitude of that undesirable behavioral impact would be great. A builder is, in essence, assessing whether the income stream from the property is likely to be adversely affected if his better plan is declared worthy of preservation some fifty to a hundred years hence and there is some use at that point that is economically preferable to preservation. The present value of income streams in the distant future is typically quite low given prevailing interest rates, and the capacity to predict which buildings will be subject to regulation in a few generations is so poor that the event may simply be ignored.

22. Buzz Thompson emphasizes this problem in relationship to the Endangered Species Act. See Barton H. Thompson Jr., "The Endangered Species Act: A Case Study of Takings and Incentives," *Stanford L. Rev.* 49 (1997): 305. Particularly in situations in which regulators give developers a long lead time before declaring particular properties off-limits rather than imposing unforeseen requirements rendering property undevelopable, citizens may rush to develop before the ban takes effect. Where, as in the case of the ESA, nondevelopment will not be ordered until a species is listed as threatened or endangered, developers aware that

regulatory demands to serve certain existing customers at lower prices may induce sellers to avoid entering ongoing buyer-seller relationships with those customers.

The critical question in each case is magnitude. Thus, for example, the ADA's demand that employers accommodate disabled workers almost surely has some disemployment effect on disabled workers, assuming (quite reasonably) that supplementary antidiscrimination norms that forbid hiring discrimination against those with disabilities are imperfectly enforceable, but the size of such disemployment effects is very difficult to discern.[23]

At times, though, regulations may better minimize adverse behavioral responses than any conceivable general tax could. Exactions, which are

---

they may own crucial, ecologically sensitive sites will be tempted to develop before regulations are put into place. In such cases, the ability of the regulators to guarantee that developers will lose nothing if the most socially valued use turns out to be nondevelopment (whether through voluntary purchase or the Takings Clause) might forestall inappropriate development.

It may be the case, though, that when developers rush to develop to evade uncompensated regulation, they heighten the regulating public's political sensitivity to problems that might otherwise escape appropriate attention. In Palo Alto today, one might argue that the appropriate decision to preserve the town's atypically large prewar housing stock was precipitated by moves toward the rapid destruction of that stock. Had the homes disappeared at a more natural pace, public awareness of the impact of the attrition may have been far lower. Moreover, at any point in time, adopting rules that would seemingly serve only to protect small numbers of homes might seem foolish. At the (natural) margin, the destruction of the homes is trivial. Only when looked at as an aggregate phenomenon, as when the rush to evade potential restriction occurs, is its importance appreciated.

23. See Peter David Blanck, "Assessing Five Years of Employment Integration and Economic Opportunity under the Americans with Disabilities Act," *Mental and Physical Disability L. Rep.* 19 (1995): 384, 386 (employment levels for the four thousand mentally retarded children and adults in Oklahoma who were the subjects of the author's ongoing longitudinal survey improved from 1989 to 1994; unemployment rates in the state generally stayed around 6.8 percent, while unemployment among the surveyed group dropped from 39 percent in 1990 to 21 percent in 1994). See also Jay Mathews, "More Disabled Hired, Census Study Shows; Federal Law Created Jobs, Access to Buildings," *Washington Post*, Jul. 26, 1996, F3 (detailed census data showed that the percentage of Americans with severe disabilities who were employed had risen from 23.3 percent in 1991 to 26.1 percent in 1994). But see S. Rosen, "Disability Accommodation and the Labor Market," in *Disability and Work: Incentives, Rights and Opportunities,* ed. C. L. Weaver (Washington, D.C.: AEI Press, 1991), 18, 22 (finding little evidence that antidiscrimination law increases employment of the disabled, though not suggesting that such legislation decreases employment). I am skeptical about whether there is as yet any good information on such disemployment effects, particularly information that distinguishes among all relevant groups of workers with disabilities. I would expect these disemployment impacts to be most significant, if they exist at all, among workers with certain forms of emotional disabilities and chronic fatigue problems who might seek work-pace and work-continuity accommodations rather than additional physical equipment.

essentially taxes negotiated ex ante with a potential developer, can be designed to capture location-specific economic rents. As a consequence, the exactions may well avoid shifts in desirable development plans or jurisdictional flight.

Naturally, the worry is that the locality will be tempted to impose exactions ex post on any supernormal profits that cannot now be earned in another jurisdiction, though doing so will create undesirable disincentives to create the supernormal profits in the first instance.[24] Imagine, for example, a store seeking a larger parking area needed to serve its atypically large and loyal customer base. The municipality might be tempted to exact concessions that strip (nearly all) the locationally specific supernormal profits (e.g., goodwill not fully transferrable to another site), though such a strategy would in fact have perverse effects on productive activity in the long run if other store owners recognized that they would be subject to confiscatory taxes if and when they needed to deal with the city (whether to expand a parking lot, extend a building, change infrastructure, and so forth).

But exactions that deliberately act as traditional tax substitutes (rather than user-fee substitutes) might not seize the supernormal profits that a party created. Ideally, these exactions should attempt to seize the supernormal profits that derive from locational rents that no particular

---

Similarly, some claim that hiring has been blunted by making it more costly to fire employees generally or some subset of employees. See, e.g., James N. Dertouzos, Elaine Holland, and Patricia Ebener, *The Legal and Economic Consequences of Wrongful Termination* (Santa Monica: Rand, 1988).

Whether the minimum wage results in high levels of disemployment, particularly among teenagers, has been the subject of enormous controversy. Compare, e.g., Finis Welch, "Minimum Wage Legislation in the United States," *Econ. Inquiry* 12 (1974): 285 (minimum wage causes substantial disemployment), with David Card and Alan B. Krueger, "Minimum Wages and Employment: A Case Study of the Fast-Food Industry in New Jersey and Pennsylvania," *Am. Econ. Rev.* 84 (1994): 772 (disemployment effects are insignificant). For an excellent critical summary, focusing especially well on nonregulatory options that might serve the purported ends of the minimum wage more effectively, see Daniel Shaviro, "The Minimum Wage, the Earned Income Tax Credit, and Optimal Subsidy Policy," *U. of Chicago L. Rev.* 64 (1997): 405.

24. The insight that government action that appears unexceptionably desirable ex post may cause problems as long as the government cannot assure actors that it will prospectively restrain from taking parallel steps in the future is most associated with Finn E. Kydland and Edward C. Prescott, "Rules Rather Than Discretion: The Inconsistency of Optimal Plans," *J. of Pol. Econ.* 85 (1977): 473. Thus, for example, expropriating any particular patent holder is efficient ex post: the invention has already been created, and charging any positive price to diffuse the information, as a patent-holding monopolist will, would result in underconsumption of the information given that diffusion has a near-zero marginal cost. But future inventors might well mistrust assurances that returns to their inventions will be protected.

landholder does anything to develop. A developer who chooses to build a subdevelopment in one (atypically desirable) political jurisdiction rather than another (less desirable) one will not be dissuaded from doing so if the tax imposed in the superior jurisdiction is not high enough to lower the value of the underlying land to him. A tax on such locational rents should, if anticipated, bear not on the developer but the landholder from whom the property is purchased. It may well be the case, though, that because the precise size of exactions is unknown ex ante, developers may often overpay for land (not receiving an appropriate discount to account for the actual typical taxing practice).[25]

Similarly, maximum price controls directed solely at scarce goods whose supply cannot reasonably increase or solely at goods that have already been produced will have an impact only on how the available goods are rationed among buyers but will not induce sellers/producers to alter their conduct. Obviously, the question of whether typical local rent-control statutes do or do not meet this description is heated.[26]

It seems clear, however, that regulations can be tailored in ways that have more or less undesirable impacts on behavior. In certain forms, a regulatory scheme may affect behavior in less troublesome ways than an equivalent general tax, while in others, the regulation's impact might be far more troubling. I understand that this claim seems to violate the standard public-finance supposition, associated with Stiglitz, that even traditional Ramsey excise taxes—levied on goods for which demand is inelastic—are less efficient than income taxes unless the excise tax is levied in such a fashion that it corrects for the leisure/work trade-off distortion inherent in an income tax (e.g., by taxing goods that are complementary to leisure and hence implicitly taxing otherwise untaxed leisure).[27]

---

25. It is then an interesting question whether developers could successfully evade exactions by arguing that they cannot afford to build at prevailing market prices or receive construction financing if charged the typical exaction. (The overpayment may be corrupt—i.e., there are effective kickbacks—or simply a function of incompetence.)

26. Compare, e.g., Richard Ault, "The Presumed Advantages and the Real Disadvantages of Rent Control," in *Rent Control: Myths and Realities,* ed. W. Block and E. Olsen (Vancouver: Fraser Institute, 1981) (opposing rent control), with Weitzman, "Economics and Rent Regulation," 975 (supporting rent control).

27. This position is described well in Joseph Stiglitz, "Pareto Efficient and Optimal Taxation and the New New Welfare Economics," in *Handbook of Public Economics,* ed. Alan Auerbach and Martin Feldstein (Amsterdam and New York: North-Holland, 1987), 991, 1023–27. Put more formally, the argument is that as long as the utility function can be separated between consumption and leisure, Pareto-efficient tax structures do not tax commodities. If the utility functions are inseparable, it would be possible, by taxing commodities for which the utility functions are inseparable, to tax higher-ability individuals without having them try to disguise themselves as lower-ability individuals.

First, though, it is not nearly so inevitable that the burden of regulations increases as income increases; in virtually any case in which a classical commodity excise tax is assessed, payers will recognize that they bear both a tax on increasing income (since they will spend some of that income on excise-taxed items) and the excise tax itself, which will have some distortionary impact on consumption decisions. It is not clear, though, that parties would or should believe each of their regulatory obligations will invariably increase if they earn more.[28]

Moreover, even in cases in which regulatory burdens (like excise tax burdens) typically increase with income, I believe that Stiglitz's argument is correct only on the highly unrealistic supposition that taxpayers both know their consumption plans at the time they make work/leisure trade-off decisions and can integrate this knowledge properly. If taxpayers do not meet these conditions, they will not treat the particular excise taxes as implicit increases in their income tax rates.[29]

Not only does Stiglitz's argument assume an unrealistically high level of foresight about how the money one earns will be used, but his argument also assumes cognitive processing capacities at odds with what I believe has been demonstrated in a good deal of cognitive psychological literature. I think there is substantial (concededly ambiguous) evidence that people solve choice problems sequentially and in a compartmentalized or bracketed manner when such problems are in some sense difficult.

People solve problems sequentially in the sense that they solve the relatively easy aspect of the whole, complex problem first and then become anchored to that solution, so that by the time they solve the second part of the problem, it is difficult to change their choices. I believe this concept is the single best explanation for such phenomena as the contrast effect, demonstrated in experiments such as one in which persons asked to choose between a Mark Cross pen, a low-quality pen, and six dollars choose the Cross pen over the money more frequently than those not offered the low-quality pen. The sequentialist account of this behavior is that the experi-

---

28. For example, the size of the optimal exaction the owner in the *Dolan* context faces does not depend on the profitability of the hardware store but on the size of the locationally specific rent. The Dolans will not, for example, face an incomelike tax on earning more profits by increasing the number of hours the store is in operation. Similarly, the losses borne by owners facing newly restrictive zoning plans are not obviously income elastic.

29. I made precisely the same argument in criticizing Shavell and Kaplow's claim in "Why the Legal System Is Less Efficient" that the income tax dominates liability rules as a redistributive mechanism (see chap. 4, n. 2) although I believe that their assumption that people will anticipate higher liability judgments in making work/leisure trade-offs is even more unrealistic than Stiglitz's assumption that parties will rationally anticipate the degree to which discretionary earnings will be partly eaten up by excise taxes.

mental subjects first choose the Cross pen over the other pen (almost instantaneously, in their minds) and then become anchored to the choice of the Cross pen before making the more difficult choice between the pen and the cash.[30]

People solve problems in a compartmentalized or bracketed fashion in the sense that they often fail to integrate two decisions that, were they integrated, would appear to a noncompartmentalizer to create an outcome identical to an alternative single decision. I believe that this is the single best explanation for the apparently irrational aspects of risk-seeking behavior of defendants in civil suits.[31] It is also the best explanation for

30. See Mark Kelman, Yuval Rottenstreich, and Amos Tversky, "Context-Dependence in Legal Decisionmaking," *J. of Legal Stud.* 25 (1996): 287, 288–89.

31. For a discussion of such risk seeking, see Jeffrey J. Rachlinski, "Gains, Losses, and the Psychology of Litigation," *Southern California L. Rev.* 70 (1997): 113. I should note that the evidence from actual market behavior that Rachlinski adduces (see pp. 150–60), would and should not wholly persuade a traditional expected-utility theorist that defendants are in fact risk seekers. Defendants may well offer settlements less than those plaintiffs are willing to accept because settling a suit with a single plaintiff may expose them to further losses, while a plaintiff will receive all of the settlement offer, net of attorney fees. Thus, imagine a suit in which the defendant believes there is a 50 percent chance of losing a hundred thousand dollars and a 50 percent chance of being exonerated; he will not offer as much as fifty thousand dollars to settle if settling will cost him an additional thirty thousand dollars in expected costs from encouraging additional plaintiffs. Rachlinski asserts such secondary costs will increase the stakes but not alter the risk analysis. The risk analysis would be unchanged only if losing the suit in court would cost an additional sixty thousand dollars in secondary costs, so that the expected value of going to trial rose by the same thirty thousand dollars. But settling and losing may or may not pose much more similar secondary costs. Furthermore, Rachlinski's claim that defendants lose a great deal as a class by failing to settle depends on his questionable assumption that they typically pay the high judgments that are reported rather than appealing or renegotiating those huge judgments that so drive his data. In a variety of ways, the experimental evidence he proffers seems less ambiguous but is subject to the typical objections to the external validity of such experimental research.

Assume, though, that defendants in litigation are risk seekers, refusing to accept settlement offers that risk-averse or risk-neutral parties would accept. They thus behave according to the descriptive dictates of prospect theory, preferring risks when they face losses from a baseline while remaining averse to risks in relationship to gains from that baseline. That behavior is not irrational, although it is not the behavior predicted by traditional expected-utility theorists who believed that people were risk averse but were decreasingly so as income increased: the fact that people's utility schemes are path dependent so that losses and gains from prior positions are asymmetrical does not violate deep rationality norms. Defendants are clearly irrational in doing so only in the limited sense that if they did not compartmentalize choices, they could increase their utility by (nearly) simultaneously settling the case and gambling with the remainder of the money at stake if they went to trial in some gambling event with lower transactions costs than a trial. Thus, rather than turn down the settlement offer of fifty thousand dollars, the risk seeker ought to accept it and gamble another fifty thousand dollars on a 50 percent odds bet paying one hundred thousand dollars 50 percent of the time. But if defendants separate the two decisions, they would be doing *two* things that

certain forms of otherwise puzzling consumption-diversification decisions.[32]

It strikes me that it is behaviorally plausible to think that people consider working more (or taking a higher-paying job) net of (relatively easily computed) income taxes or that they consider buying a more or less expensive (excise-taxed or untaxed) good but that their capacity to integrate the two decisions is limited. Such is the case in part because processing the impact of the excise tax on the work decision is simply so cognitively complex ("If I work more or take a higher-paying job, I will consume more, and some of what I will consume will be goods subject to excise taxes, unless I substitute untaxed goods for taxed goods, in which case I must still recognize that my increase in real earnings will be diminished through deadweight loss.") More important, perhaps, in terms of implicit sequencing, it seems plausible to believe that once people make their work/leisure decisions after processing income tax information, the choice to work stays anchored. In terms of compartmentalization or bracketing, it would seem most plausible that in making the decision of whether to substitute work for leisure, the fact that excise and earnings-directed taxes could be combined into a single tax on earnings will not be salient to many decision makers.

Furthermore, it is clear that an income tax that identified economic rents and taxed them more heavily than nonrent earnings would be allocatively superior to a general income tax, and regulations may function as an implicit income tax identifying rents only. Thus, though it would not be administrable, it would surely be preferable in efficiency terms to tax, for example, a professor more on her rents as a professor than on her marginal

---

cause utility loss if they followed the seemingly rational cost-minimizing strategy. First, they would accept a certain loss by settling the case; then, they would gamble seeking a gain. Defendants would simply not bracket the decision to settle and gamble as a single decision: seeking risk as to losses in the cheapest way possible. Compartmentalization may conceivably be a function of limited cognitive resources (if one is to integrate the decisions, one will have to calculate precise estimates of litigation probabilities and damage distributions, which may be very difficult); it may conceivably result from a more profound psychological tendency to divide the world into incommensurable spheres of activity.

32. Children selecting Halloween candy "diversify" their candy portfolios when offered two pieces of two distinct candies at a single house but select their favorite candy two successive times if offered one piece of candy at two successive houses, though if their desire were to diversify their candy holdings, they should do so whether the choice was simultaneous or sequential. See Daniel Read and George Lowenstein, "Diversification Bias: Explaining the Discrepancy in Variety Seeking between Combined and Separated Choices," *J. of Experimental Psychol.: Applied* 1 (1995): 34, 45–46. A visit to a single house seems to constitute the appropriate mental bracket.

consulting income (assuming higher disutility in generating that income) rather than taxing her whole income at a single rate; regulations may impose, in an approximate way, such a differentiated tax.

Still, recognition of the possible adverse allocative effects of regulation should lead to greater care in analyzing existing regulatory programs. If, for example, the ADA imposed only a uniform cost-based, per-employee accommodation requirement on all employers, the act would function, in essence, like an enterprise tax whose size was based on the number of disabled employees employed by a firm. The standard assumption is that such a tax (to the extent it were not evaded by failing to hire those with disabilities) would be borne dominantly by the firms' consumers, who would, to some modest extent, substitute goods produced by firms with fewer disabled employees for those produced by firms with more, depending on demand elasticities for the relevant goods.[33] (Firms with atypically high numbers of disabled employees compared to other firms within an industry would be expected to bear a disproportionate share of the tax. Profitability is decreased to the extent that one bears costs that do not affect typical industry costs and hence prices.) To the extent that one accepts my view that a hidden excise tax would not have an especially strong impact on work incentives, since there would be very limited recognition of the fact that one would not retain all of one's marginal earnings given the higher prices of consumed goods, this sort of implicit enterprise tax would typically have less perverse incentive effects than an increase in broad-based income taxes that might be used to fund a general governmental program to make workplaces more accessible. An implicit

---

33. If the accommodation tax were based not on the number of disabled employees but the number of workers generally, there would be no disincentive to employ workers with disabilities. In that sense, of course, one would prefer that sort of tax to a tax on employers of those with disabilities if disemployment effects were of significant magnitude. Consumers would, however, substitute goods produced by less labor-intensive firms for those that were more labor intensive, again depending on demand elasticities given relevant price changes.

But the firms would have no incentive to integrate workers with disabilities into the firm or to learn how to lower accommodation costs if the tax were a requirement to spend a certain amount accommodating however many disabled employees the firm happened to have, based on the aggregate number of employees. The ADA rightly tries to induce employers and employees with disabilities to solve the embodied employees' particular problems in working effectively given the use of the traditional, unaccommodating production technique; merely mandating that a firm spend a certain amount of money on disability-related projects (depending on the size of its workforce) may be reasonable on the implicit tax side, but it appears an extremely poor implicit spending program, providing no real incentives for employers to work to integrate people whose productive capacity is wasted in the absence of more imaginative workplace organization.

enterprise tax would, however, like any excise/retail sales tax, presumably be more regressive and hence distributively problematic.

What is both clear and significant, though, is that the ADA regulatory tax as currently formally interpreted—demanding cost-unlimited accommodations at least as long as they do not threaten the viability of the entity that bears them—acts (in theory) as a nearly 100 percent tax on profits above normal profits (those sufficient to sustain a firm's viability). Such a tax would seem, if actually imposed, to act as a considerable disincentive to earn supernormal profits (e.g., through innovation or atypically good management) and hence would seem to have extremely perverse behavioral effects. The firm is told, in essence, that if it earns supernormal profits, it must hire unlimited numbers of disabled employees, accommodating them at any cost, until all the supernormal profits are dissipated. In reality, of course, courts have not ordered hyperprofitable companies to disgorge anything resembling 100 percent of their supernormal profits to accommodate the most seriously disabled potential employees.[34]

Nonetheless, one would imagine that if one were choosing, in terms of behavioral neutrality, between an across-the-board excise tax, increases in the ordinary income tax to fund a general workplace-accessibility program, and an implicit income tax with no obvious rate limits levied on supernormal profits, the excise tax and ordinary income tax would typically cause less deadweight loss.[35] Any regulatory tax whose size varies, without any ascertainable preset limits, with firm profitability poses a considerable danger of blunting appropriate incentives both to innovate and to reduce production costs, particularly if there is a nontrivial probability that an entity will believe itself subject to the tax.

---

34. The formalistic legal explanation the courts would generally offer is that employees are not otherwise qualified if they need atypical accommodations, even though such accommodations are, formally, reasonable given that *reasonableness* is defined in terms of entity viability.

35. The concept of deadweight loss or excess burden is commonplace in analyzing explicit taxes. It refers to the difference in welfare levels that taxpayers and the tax-collecting authority would reach if taxpayers were subjected to a nonevadable head tax of the same size as the particular tax they might choose to evade and the welfare levels attained given the taxpayers' choices in a world in which the tax burden can be minimized. See, e.g., Harvey Rosen, *Public Finance,* 4th ed. (Chicago: Irwin, 1995), 303. Thus, for example, if good $X$ is subject to sales tax $T$ and good $Y$ is not, and the consumer $Z$ prefers $Y$ to $X$ at $X$'s market price + $T$ but not at $X$'s market price, then $Z$ has lost, through tax-evasion strategies, the difference in the value between goods $X$ and $Y$. That difference is less than $T$ (or the consumer would choose to pay the tax), but the tax collector does not receive $T$ since the tax is evaded: there is a deadweight loss here since no one receives that difference.

(d) Explicit taxes

The excess costs of traditional explicit taxes, while the subject of an extensive public-finance literature, are themselves no easy matter to ascertain. In weighing the choice between implicit and explicit taxes, though, one must remain aware that explicit taxes often distort behavior, though the magnitude and social costs of the changes in behavior are disputed.[36]

2.   A Brief Note on Administrative Concerns

In thinking about administrative cost concerns, it is important to recognize that it is not appropriate simply to compare the administrative costs of one of the broad-based taxes generally to the administrative costs of subjecting a party to regulation. Comparisons must be made of the marginal administrative costs that will be borne if tax proceeds are simply raised (to finance a new spending program) or if requirements are altered for the way an already-regulated party must behave to meet a new goal.[37]

---

36. If, for example, the government imposes either income or consumption taxes that fall on wages, taxpayers will, to some uncertain extent, substitute (untaxed) leisure and nonmonetized household-created commodities for (taxable) income and market-based consumption. If income (or bequests) are taxed, people will (to some uncertain extent) substitute present for future consumption. Moreover, differential taxation of capital (e.g., as a result of distinct depreciation schedules for different sorts of capital goods, capital gains treatment for some but not all investments, tax exemption of the return to investments in residential housing) may also lead to substantial misallocation of capital. Double taxation may alter behavior as well. Businesses will evade, to some extent, the corporate income tax by retaining earnings (even when the internal rate of return on the earnings is lower than the market rate of return) or by organizing outside the corporate form.

37. Naturally, there will be many situations in which a party is effectively regulated as to a certain form of conduct. It is also the case that there will be (some) situations in which the general tax that would be chosen is not simply an increase in a preexisting tax but a new or more tailored tax designed to cope with a particular problem. Thus, for example, assume that the San Jose City Council in the *Pennell* context decided to fund relief for hardship tenants not by simply increasing the existing local sales or property tax but by levying (a) a general tax on residential property owners only or on some subgroup of residential property owners who rented out their property or some subgroup of either or both these subgroups that held land whose value had changed rapidly, in the view of the taxing authority, as a result of external development that increased land rent rather than development by the parcel owners themselves; (b) an excess-profits tax on residential or all property owners, measured in any of a variety of ways; (c) a progressive income tax that had not previously existed because the city did not believe it operated other programs that were intended to redistribute from richer to poorer citizens. Inaugurating any of these complex taxes might well be costly for both taxpayers and the city bureaucracy; whether the costs would be higher than stabilizing rents for a small subset of hardship tenants is obviously difficult to say, but judgments about such administrative cost differentials will surely be germane.

It is fairly apparent that it will not typically be administratively costly to increase, marginally, the amount of funds collected through general taxes once they are in place. Taxpayers who must simply multiply their taxable base (whether it is income, real property, consumption, or whatever) by a somewhat higher number if taxes are raised will probably bear few administrative burdens.[38]

Conversely, if the state enacts a truly new regulation rather than a more stringent application of existing regulations,[39] administrative costs could be substantial. Employers or public-accommodation owners who must comply with a wholly novel regulation must themselves learn about the regulation and be monitored for compliance by a new, nontax bureaucracy. Increasing tax revenues will ordinarily therefore be a less costly revenue-raising method, in purely administrative terms, than any other option the government entity might choose to deal with a problem.

---

38. It is not entirely unambiguous that merely increasing tax rates is administratively costless. It is conceivable that as marginal rates reach some threshold (which they may reach to fund more explicit tax-and-spend programs), the advantages of minimizing the size of the taxable base grow and that efforts at reducing taxes therefore grow. These efforts are administratively costly for taxpayers and necessitate a larger state bureaucracy to counter evasion. (Even if there is no threshold, one might argue that the return to evasive activity increases continuously with increases in rates, so that more such activity would be taken.) There may well be rate thresholds for different taxpayers below which the administrative costs of evasion are not worth bearing. Beyond the threshold, though, the tax is worthwhile to evade, and once one has borne the initial fixed investment in evasion, tax compliance becomes considerably more costly for both payer and collector. Assume, for example, that a tax preparer costs one hundred dollars for his minimum chunk of time and that for that fee he can effectively understate your taxable base by a thousand dollars. Until tax rates reach 10 percent, taxpayers will not hire him, but once rates reach that level, administrative costs rise apace. (The government must try to counter his efforts. It may be worth paying him twenty dollars more to try to understate the base by an additional $250, though taxpayers would not have hired him had rates not risen to a certain point.)

It is possible, of course, not to raise marginal rates but instead to increase average rates if the revenue target increases, thereby even lowering marginal rates. This point is emphasized in Joseph Bankman and Thomas Griffith, "Social Welfare and the Rate Structure: A New Look at Progressive Taxation," *California L. Rev.* 75 (1987): 1905. Thus, increasing tax revenues may not necessitate raising marginal rates (and the concomitant advantage of evasion).

39. I do not mean to suggest that there is a clear line between new and more stringent regulatory regimes. Since, for example, developers already require building permits to proceed with development, one could presumably say that the enactment of a regulatory scheme to meet a newly perceived public end (e.g., historic preservation or maintenance of an affordable housing stock) subjects developers to a mere extension of a preexisting regime. But the relevant question is what developers must do to insure that they comply, persuade the regulatory body that they have taken adequately compliant steps, or avoid substantive compliance. Presumably, for example, hiring experts to testify about the historical insignificance of a building one wants to demolish is costly, and it is not markedly less costly because one already needed to fill out forms for a building permit.

3.   Fair Distribution of the Tax Burden

Implicit and explicit taxes are borne by different citizens. In each case, it must be determined, as best as possible, not only who pays the tax (or bears the required costs) but who ultimately bears the burdens. Whether the actual tax burden has been distributed fairly then must be judged.

For some people, the question of fairness reduces to the question of whether the proposed tax-and-spending program moves the overall distribution of income closer to an optimal level, generally evaluated according to some welfarist criterion. (Such theorists are traditionally said to attend to issues of vertical equity.) Some such welfarists believe a Rawlsian maximin distribution is to be preferred to others.[40] Some might believe the distribution must be adequately egalitarian to insure universal participation in the community's political and social culture. More traditional utilitarians might believe the marginal utility of money decreases so that greater levels of equality are always to be preferred, all else equal.

In these consequentialist views, every tax-and-spending program (implicit or explicit) is merely an opportunity for the government to redistribute income toward an optimal outcome. Most commentators who judge fairness by looking at the resulting income distribution typically assume that the tax is more desirable to the degree that it increases posttax equality, setting aside the disincentive impact of such redistributions. While there are a variety of principles to assess whether a particular post-program distribution is superior either to the preprogram distribution or to alternative postprogram ones, most judgments about taxes are simply judgments about relative progressivity, usually based on a classic utilitarian welfarist assumption that the marginal utility of income declines ex post so that parties would be risk averse ex ante.[41]

Kaplow argues that there are no coherent consequentialist distributive principles that are not in the final analysis utilitarian, at least as long as one is unwilling to disclaim the Paretian principle that any end state pre-

---

40. In such a conception, society is duty bound to maximize the welfare levels of members of the worst-off social class.

41. Naturally, a general preference for some sort of progressivity does not really answer the question of how ideal tax programs ought to be shaped: Hare, arguing against the Rawlsian maximin criterion, notes that the ideal distribution for reasonably risk-averse parties, unlike the infinitely risk-averse parties Rawls posited, might be one with a floor rather than one that maximized the income of those in the lowest class. See, e.g., R. M. Hare, "Rawls' Theory of Justice," in *Reading Rawls: Critical Studies on Rawls' A Theory of Justice*, ed. Norman Daniels (Stanford: Stanford University Press, 1989).

ferred by all parties to another end state should be adopted.[42] Kaplow's argument is straightforward. He posits situations in which every party prefers an outcome that might violate some other norms (outcome egalitarianism; horizontal equity, and so forth) and asks whether one would really willingly overrule the preference for the outcome. If not, of course, the independent principles seem to have no weight. Thus, for example, he asks whether any sort of ostensible outcome egalitarian would prefer greater income equality in a situation in which all parties preferred, at least ex ante, that the more inegalitarian outcome be chosen. Imagine, for instance, choosing between a distribution of some sum marginally less than 50 for A and marginally less than 50 for B and a 60–40 distribution, where either A or B could receive the larger share, where both parties are risk neutral and hence clearly would prefer the second distribution. All arguments that the unanimous expressed preference for the less egalitarian regime should be ignored are, in Kaplow's view, reducible to utilitarian arguments (e.g., the choice would be regretted or is the product of ex ante misperception).

The argument seems true but somewhat trivial as framed. The Paretian principle has no independent role once one incorporates the possibility of ex ante error or preference instability (regret). The fact that A and B both choose the more inegalitarian distribution has independent weight for a Paretian but not for a utilitarian, who substitutes corrected judgments of utility for ex ante ones. Thus, there is reason to doubt Kaplow's statement that individuals' "judgment may be questioned. . . . Accepting [this] criticism does not seriously affect the present argument. One could substitute 'corrected' preferences for actual preferences. . . . The policy maker could consider individuals' 'true' utility rather than perceived utility. . . . [T]he Pareto principle applied to these adjusted preferences would conflict with each anti-utilitarian norm but would be consistent with utilitarianism applied to the adjusted preferences."[43] The Pareto principle simply cannot remain a preference-based, noncontroversial individualistic principle if it is translated into a perfectionist utilitarian principle that no reform should be rejected that actually improves everyone's lot. The adjusted-preference-based utilitarian is just as willing as Kaplow's hypothetical egalitarian in a bind to seek an end state different from that which all subjects choose. Non-preference-based utilitarianism is grounded in all

---

42. See Louis Kaplow, "A Fundamental Objection to Tax Equity Norms: A Call for Utilitarianism," *Nat'l. Tax J.* 48 (1995): 497.

43. Kaplow, "Fundamental Objection," 504–5.

the sorts of vaguer justifications (egalitarianism, perfectionism, and so on) that Kaplow wants to contrast with Paretian utilitarianism. Judgments that A and B either should want or will actually come to have wanted a more egalitarian outcome because the ex post hierarchy is inconsistent with the development of appropriate community or self-respect or because equality is more consistent with some version of human flourishing are, in essence, just hedonically grounded restatements of the vague ethical principles he wants to avoid. Kaplow seems to confuse a workable utilitarianism with human-centered hedonic consequentialism: such consequentialists, like utilitarians, indeed evaluate end states depending on their impact on human happiness, but utilitarians, more narrowly, look to choice satisfaction.

Others adopt some sort of historical-process criterion in evaluating fairness. In such a view, the posttax distribution may be deemed more just to the degree that it corrects injustices that had occurred in generating the pretax distributions. Or, to take a more libertarian view, the posttax distribution is more just if it does no more than correct for rights violations that had occurred in generating the pretax distribution.

Historical-process theorists often express a preference for both regulation and user fees/benefit taxes in certain cases. In this view, it might be appropriate for parties to bear the costs of a government program, regardless of their relative wealth, insofar as they are the particular source of the problem the government seeks to ameliorate or if they benefit from the program in atypical ways. In that sense, regulation substitutes for tort law (in situations in which the plaintiff class would be too expensive to aggregate); the cost of regulatory compliance is no different, conceptually, than a tort judgment. The regulation corrects the unjust preregulatory distribution of income (the "tortfeasor's" preregulatory income is unjustly inflated because he has not had to pay the damages that he would owe except for the administrative costs of collecting them).[44]

At the same time, user fees/benefit taxes may be appropriate in cases in which there is no reason for the government to subsidize the goods and services that it happens to provide to solve coordination, nonexclusivity, or other problems that make private provision of such goods or services

---

44. Naturally, it would be best if the implicit plaintiffs benefited from the regulatory expenditures since only then would the postregulatory distribution correspond to the distribution that would have occurred in a just world, free from wrongdoing. For now, however, I focus only on the implicit tax side and hence am concerned with the disgorgement of wrongful gains rather than with compensation for wrongful losses.

impractical. In such cases, it would be unjust for the government to subsidize consumers who happen to prefer to consume goods that are provided by the state since doing so would raise these consumers' real, effective incomes above the level of those who had identical claims on consumption goods given the historical process of generating a preprogram distribution.

Fairness in the tax context has also been taken by many to require equal treatment of all those who are identically situated. This horizontal equity injunction may be empty both normatively and descriptively: no two people are really situated completely identically, and even if they were identical along all dimensions deemed relevant to taxpaying capacity, it is not clear why it would be vital to treat them the same way if there were significant gains from treating them differently. Assume, for argument's sake, that A and B were thought equal in terms of taxpaying capacity if each received the same value of commodities from their employer; assume, too, though that A received a higher portion of his compensation in the form of fringe benefits that were administratively costly to evaluate for tax-collecting purposes.[45] While there might be some reasons to tax A and B equally—for example, for efficiency reasons, it might be desirable to discourage people from overconsuming nontaxable fringe benefits—these reasons would seem simply to compete with the reasons to tax them differently (e.g., it is costly to tax A as much as B).[46]

It may well be the case that what are thought to be intuitions to treat equals equally are actually stand-ins for more particular prudential judgments. For example, one may believe that it is inefficient to tax similarly situated parties differently, since doing so will lead people to substitute untaxed for taxed activities, breaching standard norms against allocative

45. For these purposes, I ignore the difficulty of assessing whether two taxpayers should be judged equal when the cost of providing compensation is equal or when the market values of the goods the employees receive are the same: are two taxpayers similarly situated when each receives the same money salary but one also receives goods with zero or very low marginal cost of provision to that particular employer (e.g., an airline employee given the right to use empty seats on flights)?

46. See Louis Kaplow, "Horizontal Equity: Measures in Search of a Principle," *Nat'l. Tax J.* 4 (1989): 139.

As a practical matter, injunctions to attend to horizontal equity often are interpreted to mean that government programs (including tax programs) ought not reverse the rank order of citizens' pretax/preprogram utility positions. See, e.g., Martin Feldstein, "On the Theory of Tax Reform," *J. of Pub. Econ.* 6 (1976): 77, 79; A. B. Atkinson, "Horizontal Equity and the Distribution of the Tax Burden," in *The Economics of Taxation,* ed. Henry Aaron and Michael Boskin (Washington, D.C.: Brookings Institution, 1982). But such a translation of the horizontal equity norm is highly problematic. First, it implies that even trivial utility reversals are far more significant than massive alterations in the size distribution of income. Thus, for example, assume the pretax distribution of income is 100, 10, 9: the injunction to

inefficiency.[47] One might also believe that a polity that can draw arbitrary distinctions among taxpayers or among program beneficiaries will enact programs that favor particular interest groups, without regard to the social benefits of such programs.[48] Similarly, general norms against arbitrariness may help enforce norms against discrimination on the basis of membership in socially disadvantaged castes. It may be more difficult to prove legislative hostility or even indifference to members of a socially disadvantaged group than to forbid programs in which particular citizens are treated worse without any obvious justification.[49] Arbitrary taxes might be unpredictable as well, and to the degree that citizens are risk averse and hence prefer a state in which they are able to predict posttax income with less dispersion, the imposition of such taxes might decrease utility.[50] Finally, as noted in my prior discussion of equal protection in taxation, horizontal equity norms may stand in for norms against undue govern-

---

attend to horizontal equity implies that a posttax distribution of 102, 8.9, 8.91 is highly problematic, while distributions of 11, 10, 9 or 60, 50, 9 are not. See Kaplow, "Horizontal Equity." One might choose instead to attend not just to reversals but the level of movement of all parties from their status quo ante position (measuring not so much reversals as the resemblance of pre- and posttax distributions). See Harvey S. Rosen, "An Approach to the Study of Income, Utility, and Horizontal Equity," *Q. J. of Econ.* 98 (1978): 307, for an index that attempts to achieve this goal. By measuring level of movement, though, horizontal equity norms seem to forbid precisely what vertical equity may demand (increases in equality that make the pre- and posttax distributions dissimilar). Second, and more important, any norm that emphasizes the importance of maintaining the pretax distribution implies that the status quo ante has some normative force that it simply does not deserve.

    47. Kaplow, "Horizontal Equity," 149.

    48. Joseph Stiglitz, "Utilitarianism and Horizontal Equity: The Case for Random Taxation," *J. of Pub. Econ.* 18 (1982): 1. Presumably, this idea is troublesome both because governmental entities should adopt only cost-justified programs and because of the worry that, to some uncertain extent, interest groups will waste undue resources in seeking distributive transfers if such narrow programs are available. This second apprehension is basic to those who fear the formation of a rent-seeking society and attribute slowdowns in productivity growth to the attractiveness of rent seeking. See generally Mancur Olson, *The Rise and Decline of Nations* (New Haven: Yale University Press, 1982), and James M. Buchanan, Robert D. Tollison, and Gordon Tullock, eds., *Toward a Theory of the Rent-Seeking Society* (College Station: Texas A&M University, 1980).

    49. See, e.g., Richard Musgrave, "Optimal Taxation, Equitable Taxation, and Second-Best Taxation," *J. of Pub. Econ.* 6 (1976): 3.

    50. Kaplow, "Horizontal Equity," 145–46. See also G. Brennan, "Horizontal Equity: An Extension of an Extension," *Public Finance* 26 (1971): 437. The idea that a violation of horizontal equity in taxation is essentially equivalent to undue risk imposition may motivate the belief that the Takings Clause should be understood as mandating publicly provided insurance against the risk of unexpected government actions that alter the value of owners' holdings. The question then arises of whether there are significant market failures in the provision of insurance against takings that make it appropriate for the state to insure against its own conduct rather than to expect risk-averse private parties to do so. The insurance perspective

mental privacy intrusions. Justifying what might otherwise seem to be arbitrary distinctions in treatment between individuals might depend on state authorities knowing details of citizens' lives (their preferences, their responsiveness to particular taxing schemes) that could be discovered only by detailed inquiry into their plans and feelings. The desire to protect citizens' impersonal relationship with the public bureaucracy may in part motivate the preference for having tax burdens turn only on a small number of readily publicly observable facts.

It is plausible that the conventional taxes will typically dominate all other methods of government conduct in terms of these underlying horizontal equity concerns, whether allocative efficiency, interest group capture,[51] discrimination, risk imposition,[52] or impersonality. But it is important to recall that conventional taxes are hardly immune from these problems.

People frequently worry about restrictive regulations on the development of vacant land.[53] From the vantage point of those who have already developed, an empty lot is frequently most valuable left empty (as a greenspace, no-noise, no-congestion buffer), though it is dubious whether the

---

on takings was initially embodied in Lawrence Blume and Daniel L. Rubinfeld, "Compensation for Takings: An Economic Analysis," *California L. Rev.* 72 (1984): 569; and Kaplow, "Economic Analysis of Legal Transitions," 509. Kaplow alone emphasized the degree to which risk-averse parties ordinarily would be expected to insure privately unless there were reasons to suspect that such a private market would fail.

51. In subsequently discussing political-process issues, I will examine in more detail whether taxes are inherently less likely to be imposed on insular subgroups (identified on the basis of ascriptive traits or not). I have already discussed the issue of whether conventional taxes are atypically efficient, noting that it is certainly possible to tailor regulations that are atypically unlikely to misallocate resources.

52. As a general matter, risk is imposed by taxes or by regulation both when citizens are uncertain about how norms will apply to particular cases because there is no general rule and when citizens are unsure about their factual circumstances. I suspect some commentators overestimate the degree to which certain forms of regulation pose unique risks because these scholars are thinking only of legal uncertainty. The risk inherent in regulations like exactions is of the first sort and may well be more obvious; there is no rule that describes how much will be exacted given some obvious features of the taxpayer's situation. Similarly, the prototypical isolated taking of a parcel implements a rule in only the loosest sense (one's property will be taken if needed), but the rule cannot help predict whether property will be needed based on its observable characteristics. But perfectly certain, perfectly general rules can generate just as much factual risk. One may know that taxes will be set at 10 percent of assessed value on houses purchased after the year 2000 (an observable feature of the home, specified in the statute) and at only 5 percent on those purchased before then but know so little about the likelihood of purchasing after 2000 that estimates of expected lifetime posttax income are just as dispersed as they would be if the only risk were expropriation based on unannounced or unannounceable factors.

53. This is the main substantive theme in William A. Fischel, *Regulatory Takings: Law, Economics, and Politics* (Cambridge: Harvard University Press, 1995), esp. 52–53, 278, 282, 287–88.

empty lot is worth enough to those who have already developed to bid more for a nondevelopment servitude than would-be users would bid.[54] Given this situation, those who own already-developed property, the typical voters in local elections, might simply choose to regulate against development without offering compensation. Those who suggest more vigorous policing of such problematic regulatory takings suggest that they are most vulnerable once it is recognized that they violate horizontal equity norms that would forbid treating taxpayers differently depending on when they acquired property.[55] Substantively, of course, these regulations may indeed burden newcomers in ways for which these horizontal equity norms may stand in. There might be a form of undue capture by a dominant and identifiable group, status-based discrimination (if newcomers are different), or burdens on protected rights (of mobility) or inefficiency (if the local government rejects a more efficacious means of meeting an end because doing so spreads the burden more broadly).

But the idea that regulation uniquely poses these problems seems farfetched. The municipality might well charge substantial user fees for new infrastructure while having provided and maintaining the infrastructure for existing owners out of general funds. Similarly, the government might selectively impose an inaction strategy by refusing to extend services to those who would live in new developments that are (at least arguably) similarly situated to the old-timers' developments (e.g., traffic lights to ease exiting a subdevelopment might not be built even though such lights have been maintained in similar situations; the city might not build a conveniently located school or acquire nearby parkland although the community is generally filled with parks).[56] Arguably though, the nondevelopment strategy is most immune to

---

54. A standard rationale for demanding compensation is that it forces the legislature to determine whether the proposed regulation is genuinely efficient. It is efficient if and only if the legislature is willing to pay as much to obtain the regulatory end state as someone else would pay to avoid it. For classic discussions, see, e.g., Blume and Rubinfeld, "Compensation," 569, 620–23; Thomas J. Miceli and Kathleen Segerson, "Regulatory Takings: When Should Compensation Be Paid?" *J. of Legal Stud.* 23 (1994): 749, 753–54; Joseph L. Sax, "Takings and the Police Power," *Yale L. J.* 74 (1964): 36, 62–67.

55. Whether these regulations genuinely violate some workable general norm against treating equals unequally is dubious. Given the fact that the marginal cost of development generally exceeds its average cost given escalating congestion, the regulated and unregulated parties are not obviously similarly situated. For the standard account of increasing congestion costs, see George S. Tolley, "The Welfare Economics of City Bigness," *J. of Urb. Econ.* 1 (1974): 324.

56. On the spending side, municipal decisions might also favor insiders over newcomers, and taxes might be raised a good deal to fund services of little or no moment to the newcomers. A general tax-and-spend program to finance an expensive restoration of a historic district might effectively transfer funds from general taxpayers (of whom a significant number might be newcomers) to a subgroup of long-time residents living near the historic district.

democratic counterpressure. Once the old residents allow development, they will have to face a significant number of countervoters, while there may be a very small number of owners of undeveloped parcels as long as development is thwarted, but it is easy to construct completely plausible scenarios in which (relatively) isolated, (relatively) small communities are just as vulnerable as isolated parcel owners.[57]

## Generating Benefits: A Catalog of the Basic Options

The government may generate benefits by providing a valued service either directly or by inducing others to perform that service by paying them to do so (privatized state service delivery) or providing funds for the direct consumers of the goods to pay them for doing so (vouchers). In all three of these cases the state has adopted a tax-and-spend program. The state might also mandate that a private party provide the relevant service for free or, if the party provides the service in any case, that it do so at controlled prices. In both these cases, the state has adopted a regulatory option.[58] The government may also generate benefits by forbidding certain

---

57. Conventional taxes have certainly not been immune to the substantive problems that those concerned with horizontal equity typically emphasize, though every substantive problem does not arise each time there is a breach of the horizontal equity norms.

Property taxes, for example, historically covered both real and personal property but by the early twentieth century bore almost exclusively on real property. While such differential treatment of real and personal property might well be inefficient (leading to overinvestment in personal property) or even pose group-capture problems (to the uncertain extent that those who held land were differentiable in politically salient ways from other citizens), it is unlikely that this treatment posed problems of undue risk imposition, group-based discrimination, or undue intrusiveness. (On the contrary, one of the bases for the attack on personal property taxation was that it was incompatible with unintrusive administration.) Distinctions, though, in rates or exemptions within the class of real property (e.g., late-1970s tax revolters' distinctions in such enactments as Proposition 13 between old and new homeowners; distinctions between tax rates on farm and urban land that were more prevalent in the first third of the twentieth century) may be far more problematic in terms of interest-group politics and perhaps even (at least mild levels of) risk imposition (on the assumption that it is more difficult to predict how mobile one is likely to be than the value of the property one is likely to own). For a fuller discussion of the history of property taxation, see Glenn Fisher, *The Worst Tax? A History of the Property Tax in America* (Lawrence: University Press of Kansas, 1996).

58. Thus, for example, the government could itself retrofit public accommodations to make them accessible to people with particular mobility limitations, hire private firms to do so, order public-accommodation owners to do so but compensate them for their expenditures, or simply order public accommodation owners to do so. (As I note later, compensation may be tendered for actual expenditures, on a cost-plus or cost-only basis, or for typical expenditures that would be needed to meet the regulatory mandate, which would be equivalent to the loss in market value of the property if the regulated party bore all of the costs of

conduct in which a party would otherwise engage that makes some or all other citizens worse off (e.g., building above a certain height or destroying historically significant buildings). Again, the government may avert unwanted conduct through a tax-and-spend method, paying parties to forbear from such conduct either by purchasing negative servitudes ex ante or compensating for the regulatory taking ex post. The government could also adopt the regulatory option, simply forbidding the conduct without compensation.[59]

There is an extensive literature reviewing the choice between public provision and private provision of services. Advocates of increasing levels of privatization of even those services that would remain monopolized (e.g., prisons, electric utilities) frequently argued that the state would be better off contracting with profit-seeking bidders to provide services. Such advocates highlight the extent to which profit seekers have strong incentives to reduce service delivery costs to maximize the spread between revenues and costs, while public providers will lower costs only insofar as they fear they may bump up against loose budget constraints dictated by political resistance to tax increases.[60] Opponents of privatization focused on

---

meeting the mandate.) The first three involve taxing and spending; the last is traditional regulation. I suppose one could even imagine a system in which those who made services available for customers with disabilities could charge them some of the costs of providing those services with a regulated maximum price, but I do not think price regulation meets any of the genuine regulatory aims here.

59. There will also be ambiguous cases in which a goal could be met through forbearance or through service provision. For example, a private party could meet a requirement to maintain water quality in a certain area by failing to use the water or by purifying it after use (and the state could compensate or not for the costs borne in either case). Requirements that habitats be preserved to maintain the population levels of particular species might be met by nondevelopment or through conduct that compensates for otherwise harmful changes in the initially favorable environment. Thus, for example, a utility might protect the ozone layer by complying with regulations demanding burning of less coal or cleaner coal or by engaging in compensatory reforestation projects.

60. For some standard arguments favoring privatization, see generally, Emanuel S. Savas, *Privatization: The Key to Better Government* (Chatham: Chatham House, 1987); Anthony E. Boardman and Aidan R. Vining, "Ownership and Performance in Competitive Environments: A Comparison of the Performance of Private, Mixed, and State-Owned Enterprises," *J. of L. and Econ.* 32 (1989): 1. Some economists who are generally wary of the capacity of government enterprises to perform effectively attribute much of this slack to their immunity from competition. See, e.g., Douglas W. Caves and Laurits R. Christensen, "The Relative Efficiency of Public and Private Firms in a Competitive Environment: The Case of Canadian Railroads," *J. of Pol. Econ.* 88 (1980): 958. Conversely, others believe that perverse managerial incentives in the public sector lead state-firm managers to deviate more from a wealth-maximizing strategy than do private firm owners, regardless of the levels of market competition, thereby causing lower rates of productivity growth in state firms even in cases in which

the state's difficulty in monitoring service-provision quality and the provider's perverse incentives to reduce service quality if doing so would reduce cost, given these monitoring problems. Opponents also frequently note that most of the private entities' cost advantages could be achieved by the state if it chose to engage in social-welfare-destructive, wage-minimizing strategies.[61]

Advocates of privatization have been even more fervent in urging that state monopolies be replaced by competitive private providers or a mix of competing private and public providers whenever it is feasible to employ multiple providers. Thus, for example, public schools could be replaced by a mix of private and public schools that competed for consumers' patronage,[62] though the state might still fund (as much) school spending (as it currently does) through vouchers that gave each family the equivalent of its share of the current school budget.[63] But the conflict between those who urge the continuation of state provision monopolies and those who urge that vouchers be given for use in purchasing privately provided services is not, in the final analysis, directly germane to the choice between regulation and taxing and spending: all of these programs are tax-and-spend programs.

The literature is germane though, to the extent to which it is persuasive in arguing that in at least some cases dispersed private profit-maximizing providers are more cost-effective than a monopolistic government

---

static productivity levels are comparable to those in private firms. See Isaac Ehrlich, Georges Gallais-Hamonno, Zhiqiang Liu, and Randall Lutter, "Productivity Growth and Firm Ownership: An Analytical and Empirical Investigation," *J. of Pol. Econ.* 102 (1994): 1006.

61. See, e.g., Paul Starr, "The Limits of Privatization," in *Prospects for Privatization,* ed. Steve H. Henke (New York: Academy of Political Science, 1987), 124; Joseph F. Field, "Making Prisons: An Improper Delegation of a Governmental Power," *Hofstra L. Rev.* 15 (1987): 649, 663 n. 115 (private prison companies would be free to hire nonunion workers at less money than the wages paid to union staff).

62. For a standard argument that such a system would improve the quality of school services, see Myron Lieberman, *Privatization and Educational Choice* (New York: St. Martin's Press, 1989), 152–229.

63. Vouchers would be set at the pro rata share only on the incorrect assumption that spending levels do not vary per pupil; naturally, though, it would be necessary to give families whose children received costlier services (e.g., special-education-eligible pupils) higher vouchers if the goal were to alter only the service provision side rather than the subsidy to users.

In a similar fashion, public housing could be replaced by vouchers permitting parties to buy or lease privately owned units. The postal monopoly could admit competitors but continue to operate, or the government could get out of the mail-delivery business altogether and subsidize those users who might suffer in what the state feels is an unacceptable fashion if forced to bear full market costs for mail delivery.

provider with a relatively loose budget constraint to induce cost-cutting, for it will always be the case that when regulation rather than direct provision of services is chosen, services will be provided by dispersed private providers (most of whom will be profit-motivated entities). Thus, if it is believed that dispersed private providers will deliver accessibility services more cost-effectively than the state or even a handful of private entities with which the state contracts to do retrofitting, particularly since the optimal strategies for service delivery may so radically differ among establishments, then forcing private parties to deliver these services may mean that they will be created more cost-effectively. Public-accommodation owners should compete (in cost terms) to meet regulatory demands most efficaciously; minimizing production costs, whether mandated or not, will increase firm profitability. Of course, though, dispersed private providers could be forced to provide services, just as they are under classic regulatory schemes, but be compensated for the costs they bear, or the state could contract with a wide range of bidders to provide services, so that a simple preference for dispersed provision does not really dictate a preference for uncompensated regulation.

To make that argument, one must believe not only that the private party will (at least sometimes) provide the services more efficiently than would a public provider but that in the event that the party is compensated for providing the services, some of these efficiency advantages will be lost. Imagine in this regard that the state is deciding whether to compensate (a) service providers,[64] (b) those ordered to forbear from certain conduct, and (c) parties who might meet regulatory goals either through forbearance or conduct.[65]

---

64. The example I will continue to use is public-accommodation owners who must retrofit their buildings to increase access opportunities for people who are physically unable to use the buildings in their current form.

65. An example on which one might focus is a regulatory requirement to preserve a viable habitat that stabilizes the population of an endangered species. This requirement might be met through either nondevelopment or compensatory conduct.

I do not discuss in the text the price-control cases. Presumably, though, advocates of the most prominent price-control program—rent control—believe that the program is more efficacious than the standard tax-and-spend alternative (vouchers) in gaining continued access to housing for current occupants, assuming that the dominant goal of such statutes is to allocate housing to current occupants when they could no longer afford market rates. (The fact that current occupants are typically not allowed to sublet at market rates implies that this effort does not seek to redistribute income to tenants in possession but to preserve certain sorts of public goods: neighborhood stability or a particular class mix in a jurisdiction.)

Imagine, too, in the first and last case, that the government (a) compensates on a cost-plus basis, (b) compensates only for costs that are actually borne, or (c) compensates without regard to the particular costs the entity bears but rather more typical ones (the decline in the market value of the relevant property or business caused by the initial enactment of a completely unanticipated regulation). In the second, pure forbearance case, it would appear that the state would compensate, if it were to compensate, only on the third basis (the decline in market value that occurred when the unanticipated regulation was enacted). Compensation should be expected to pose distinct problems in the three classes of cases. I believe that the problems would typically be most severe in cases in which the private entities must—or might—actively provide services to meet some public goal.

## (a) Cost-plus and pure cost compensation

The difficulties with cost-plus compensation schemes are familiar, largely from the Department of Defense's experience with cost overruns and inefficient weapons procurement.[66] While it is theoretically possible for auditors to determine that the private entity has spent more than a reasonable amount producing the good or delivering the service for which the government agrees to pay, the monitoring state will always be fighting against the entity's perverse incentives to increase the cost of service provision. If the profit level is set at a percentage of costs, the incentive of the entity both to

---

From the vantage point of rent-control proponents, vouchers will do little good. The supply of housing in a particular area is inelastic in the moderately long run, so that price is simply set by the demand price of the marginal buyer seeking housing. Giving vouchers to some subset of poor housing consumers will simply inflate the market price further but cannot induce the construction of more units (which, by hypothesis, cannot be created in the moderately short run).

66. For classic discussions of cost-plus-fixed-fee (CPFF) contracts and variants, such as redeterminable fixed-price contracts and incentive contracts (in which sellers and the government share the risks of cost overruns), see Frederic M. Scherer, *The Weapons Acquisition Process: Economic Incentives* (Boston: Div. of Research, Graduate School of Business Administration, Harvard University, 1964), 132–40, 184–90, 268–70, 313–25 (mechanisms to attain efficiency at both design phase and production phase are largely ineffective in reducing costs; though firms do compete with producers of close substitute weapon systems and compete for budgetary allocations, they do so largely by trying to increase performance quality); J. Ronald Fox, *Arming America: How the U.S. Buys Weapons* (Cambridge: Harvard University Press, 1974), 165–68, 231–32 (cost overruns were widespread, incentives to reduce costs were weak under CPFF systems and variants thereof).

increase actual costs and overstate what it has spent is most obvious.[67] Thus, if the government agrees to pay a retrofitting public-accommodation owner whatever is spent to retrofit plus some percentage of the amount spent, it will be especially administratively difficult to stop the owner from increasing spending. If landholders could receive a particular level of compensation to let their land remain undeveloped but could receive a good deal more if they spent money to restore the property to a species-preserving state, they may choose development and restoration though it is socially more costly.

A firm's profit from complying with some regulatory mandate could obviously be set at a constant dollar level rather than as a percentage of spending. Such a cost-plus scheme would seem, at first blush, to function just like a simple cost-compensation scheme. It would appear to provide no incentives to reduce expenditures and in that sense would seem to be dominated by uncompensated schemes in which the incentives to reduce expenditures would be strong,[68] but it would not seemingly provide any obvious incentives to increase them. Assuming the rate of return on capital in alternative projects is greater than zero, increasing input expenditures in situations in which one will not receive added profits is ordinarily undesirable. But the firm does not increase expenditures using its own capital when it receives compensation for costs or compensation for costs plus some fixed dollar amount; the government ex post provides a no-interest loan, available solely for these purposes. Moreover, as Scherer notes, firms' opportunity costs in utilizing highly specialized human and physical capital are often low during procurement downturns, and keeping an inventory of, for example, engineers fully employed when unneeded may redound to the firm's long-term benefit.[69]

In practice, the incentives may be even more perverse. First, those who worry that managers are imperfectly monitored by profit-seeking shareholders have long been concerned that managers may tend to maxi-

---

67. Such costs-plus-a-percentage-of-costs contracts were used in military procurement in World War I but were thought so prone to abuse that they were banned both by the First War Powers Act of 1941 (P.L. 354, 77th Cong. [55 Stat. 838–39]) and the Armed Service Procurement Act of 1948 (10 U.S.C. 2306 [a]).

68. There is a moral-hazard problem in insuring service providers fully for the losses they will actually sustain in service provision; there is little reason for them to minimize these losses.

69. See Scherer, *Weapons Acquisition Process,* 184–88. Moreover, the firm may be able to allocate its high indirect costs to a contract if its direct costs rise and may be able to justify higher cost estimates on future contracts. See Fox, *Arming America,* 232.

mize the size of the entity they manage to enhance prestige or power, making expenditure increases desirable.[70] Where, as here, shareholders are not in conflict with managers whose selfish interest is to increase the size of the budgets (and presumably staff) that they control, it would appear reasonable to fear unwarranted spending. Second, it may be possible for the firm as an entity or individuals within the firm to benefit selfishly from the expenditures that are recompensed, even though these expenditures ostensibly benefit only outsider third-party contractors. Auditors may be unable to identify all instances of explicit or implicit selfish appropriation of overcharges and overspending. Thus, for example, if the retrofitting public-accommodation owner pays an outside contractor unduly high fees to build a ramp but receives direct or indirect kickbacks or the contractor is related in some sense either to the entity or to individual managers therein, the retrofitting entity's decision makers will not be indifferent between both spending and receiving more and spending and receiving the lowest possible amount needed to provide the relevant accommodations. Finally, any cost-based compensation system generates considerably more administrative costs than does an uncompensated system,[71] since reviewing claims will inevitably be costly.

### (b) Compensating based on typical losses

If the state chooses to compensate an owner who must or may provide a service to generate relevant benefits based on the projected costs a typical owner is expected to bear, there will be (generally) desirable incentives to reduce actual spending levels below the projected typical rates. The state might adjust compensation rates downward once it sees that entities can meet goals more cheaply than initially believed, wiping out the firm's gains from becoming more efficient than the state had predicted. Still, it seems implausible that nonconspiring entities would fail to try to achieve cost

---

70. The classic work suggesting that managers seek to maximize enterprise size rather than profits is William Baumol, *Business Behavior, Value and Growth* (New York: Macmillan, 1959). For a typical skeptical response suggesting that performance matters at least as much as size in determining managerial compensation, see, e.g., Frank H. Easterbrook, "Managers' Discretion and Investors' Welfare: Theories and Evidence," *Delaware J. of Corp. L.* 9 (1984): 540, 560–62.

71. Obviously, as Michelman noted long ago, compensation is always costly: in his calculus, one pays compensation when and only when these administrative costs are lower than the demoralization costs that would occur in the absence of compensation. For now, my point is simply to note that, in prudential terms, a system of compensating service providers will require a cost-control bureaucracy.

savings simply to avoid disclosing otherwise private information about minimum service-provision costs. Each firm can hope to benefit by being (relatively) uniquely efficacious, and each will know it will be harmed if others disclose their efficaciousness through cost-cutting conduct whether or not the firm that is considering cutting costs actually attempts to cut costs: failing to cut costs is thus a reasonable strategy only if all entities coordinate the strategy. Assuming, then, that cost-reducing incentives would work, one still must ask whether they would be desirable. They should, at least as long as the regulator can monitor the quality of service provision to insure that the party has not reduced costs by reducing quality. (Naturally, though, a precisely parallel monitoring problem besets regulators who do not compensate at all, since the parties they regulate will have an identical interest in reducing compliance costs.)

But if there are substantial variations between the relevant settings or substantial uncertainty before the fact about what costs will be generated, the administrative costs of determining an appropriate figure will be enormous. Homogeneous regulated parties will tend to overstate projected costs to administrative agencies, which would presumably typically have less information than the parties about their least-cost regulatory options. Though the social costs of service provision will not obviously increase if the regulated parties are systematically overcompensated, the state will spend (and therefore tax) more than it must to obtain the desired benefits. The excess taxation doubtless creates needless efficiency losses. Moreover, there will be excess rent-seeking entry into those industries where overcompensation is greatest.[72] To the degree that the regulated parties are sig-

---

72. It appears that in the cases I have described, overcompensation will act as a lump-sum subsidy with no impact on marginal costs and hence will not lower prices for the products produced by the regulated party. In such a case, short-run excess profits and rent-dissipating entry would be expected. For an exploration of a market in which the persistent availability of excess profits leads to dissipation of such rents through excess, wasteful entry, see Ian Ayres, "Further Evidence of Discrimination in New Car Negotiations and Estimates of Its Cause," *Michigan L. Rev.* 94 (1995): 109, 144–45 (sellers charge African American and female buyers a price closer to the buyers' reservation price than to sellers' costs; the excess profit that the sellers can earn is not dissipated by competition from other sellers willing to offer lower prices but leads to excessive entry into the car dealership market). However, if considering a compensation scheme that subsidized the provision of each unit sold (e.g., by requiring a safety feature attached to each good whose cost of installation would be overpaid for by the state), the effects would be more complex. If the subsidy were uniform, it should be passed along to consumers of the good, and the adverse efficiency effect would simply be the unwarranted substitution of this good for other products that were not subsidized. If the subsidy varied, some firms would still earn excess profits, and rent-dissipating entry would still be expected.

nificantly heterogenous, establishing an appropriate schedule of payments also will be difficult, and a random pattern of subsidies and penalties to competitive firms might well distort capital flow. The biggest problem, though, whether producers are homogeneous or heterogeneous, is that they may well find that the greatest return on investment they can receive is not the return to cost-effective innovation in service delivery but investment in hiring various advocates to overstate effectively the appropriate compensation rate: not only must the deadweight loss from these unproductive investments be accounted for, but the state will also have to spend more to counter overstated claims, knowing they will be well supported by consulting engineers and their attorney spokespeople.

Seemingly, compensation poses the fewest direct, nonadministrative efficiency costs when the state achieves desired benefits by demanding that parties forbear from particular conduct. Parcel owners forbidden to build above a certain height simply cannot obtain the relevant benefits more cheaply than by the method they are ordered to use. It is true that compensating them for the typical costs of compliance (the drop in market value of the property from unzoned to zoned state) might cause some moral-hazard problems, but it is dubious whether such effects will be significant. Compensating an owner for a typical parcel-specific taking (e.g., seizing the fee to build a road) indeed makes it more likely, at the margin, that owners will not reduce social losses by minimizing development even when the probability of eminent domain increases. Similarly, owners of parcels ultimately subject to a building-height restriction may be unduly indifferent to whether they take steps that increase the spread between the unzoned and zoned value of the parcels if they are fully insured against that loss. One can readily hypothesize examples of these sorts of steps: developers might develop part of their property so that scenic views would be blocked if only the short buildings permitted by the zoning plan were built elsewhere on the land; developers might prepare land or build foundations or other infrastructure that would sustain high-rise development but are unnecessary for permitted buildings and receive compensation that reflects the fact that the land is, in the absence of regulation, especially suited for high-rise development. But it is far less clear that the magnitude of the actual moral-hazard problem is large enough to be of concern. It is obvious as well that the need to compensate generates transactions costs; whether or not owners take steps that increase the actual spread between regulated and unregulated value, they will surely attempt to overstate what that spread is (expending resources to do so persuasively), and the state will expend resources first countering and then adjudicating these exaggerated claims.

One suspects, though, that the most persuasive reason not to compensate in the pure forbearance cases is distributive rather than efficiency oriented, based on the supposition that the demand for forbearance precludes the parcel owner from impoverishing others unjustly through activity that is privately advantageous. Compensation is generally provided in the opposite circumstances—when society has unduly impoverished the parcel owner for its own collective advantage.

# CHAPTER 5

# Prudential Concerns (II): Political Process

There are two typical process-based attacks on the use of regulation. First, regulations are thought to be unduly opaque to voters: since they know neither who is really paying for nor who is receiving the benefits of the regulatory scheme, the programs are not adequately scrutinized. Second, critics of regulation fear that it is all too easy to unduly focus the costs of regulatory compliance on narrow, relatively politically powerless constituencies rather than the population as a whole. Thus, in process terms, voters will not scrutinize whether the benefits of the regulation outweigh compliance costs, since most voters know they will not bear any of these costs. I believe those voicing these concerns quite seriously overstate both the transparency and the inevitable breadth of most tax-and-spending programs. Those expressing these concerns may also mildly understate the distributive transparency of regulation.

The claim that broad public-mindedness can radically be encouraged by mandating tax-and-spend programs seems extremely peculiar. The two sorts of rent-seeking constituencies that have typically received the most attention—those soliciting localist pork-barrel legislation and interest-group entitlement mongers—traditionally seek tax-financed, legislatively appropriated expenditures, for example, public-works projects or indexed Social Security grants, rather than regulatory beneficence. Moreover, the idea that there is either significant fiscal illusion or a bureaucratic bias to regulate more and spend less is dubious. If one believes bureaucrats are less public-minded than self-regarding, it is plausible that they seek to maximize budgets rather than regulatory efficacy.[1]

There is, though, in my view, a more serious process concern that leads me to be rather critical of some fairly uncontroversial regulatory programs.

---

1. I do not mean to dismiss the idea that in a political climate hostile to taxation and wary of deficit financing, there is political pressure on legislators to satisfy constituent demands through unfunded regulatory mandates. I simply believe that this pressure is both counterbalanced in part and less determinative of behavior than those who focus on its salience may believe.

While regulation may, on many occasions, be the best governmental option for pragmatic efficiency reasons, it is common within this political culture to believe, mistakenly, that parties are (and should be) regulated only when they are, in a moralistic sense, wrongdoers or rights violators.

This moralistic view of regulation can lead to two suboptimal results. First, society may refuse to regulate even when doing so would entail fewer social costs (e.g., monitoring costs) than the tax-and-spend alternative because the party to be regulated is not viewed as a wrongdoer. The second point, however, is more important: the moralistic view of regulation may lead to overregulation. The sense that the regulation's beneficiaries have a right to be free from wrongdoing by the regulated party precludes analysis of whether the costs of the implicit spending program the regulation enacts are justified compared to alternative spending programs.

Assume, for example, that public-accommodation owners rather than the state are required to provide services to those with mobility impairments dominantly to limit the costs of providing a certain level of access. If, though, it is nonetheless widely believed that the costs can be imposed on private parties only because the failure to provide such access is a rights violation, the disabled will be believed to have a superior, higher-priority, rights-based claim to social resources than they ought to have. Had the state directly provided the services, justifying their provision as a mechanism for collectively meeting need (including the group-specific need for social inclusion as well as the more individualistic need for more consumer goods), the decision to expend funds on the services would, in my view, more likely be seen to compete with decisions to fund programs that would benefit other needy citizens.

In this view, the cultural problem is that each form of government action has an accepted, ideal-typical set of characteristic functions. Instead of recognizing that each form of government action can and does meet all the characteristic functions, depending on the setting in which it is employed, and that the choice among forms of action may (or should) be made on purely prudential grounds, the action-types tend to be reified. It is common to ascribe general features to each act of regulation or each act of taxation without regard to its actual, more particularized role.

### The Usual Case against Uncompensated Regulations and Its Discontents

Those who would attempt to induce governmental entities to use tax-and-spending programs rather than to regulate to improve legislative functioning generally make four basic arguments. They argue first that the regulatory tax base may be unduly narrow compared to the bases that would be employed if the entity were forced to use tax-and-spending programs. Giving governmental entities the option of concentrating costs on subgroups compromises their capacity to do reasonable cost-benefit calculations about the programs they enact, since one group (the politically dominant) will receive the benefits, while another group, whose welfare the beneficiaries may discount, will bear the costs. In this regard, the problem with regulatory taxation is that it is all too obvious how its benefits and burdens are distributed so that those with legislative power (whether majorities or a minority group distinct from those targeted to comply with regulatory mandates) see the distributive pattern clearly and enact poor legislation. Legislative bodies would improve their deliberative capacity to assess legislation if the beneficiaries and victims of legislation were always either the same people, randomized samples of the same group, or altruistically linked. At the very least, situations should be avoided in which a group imposes burdens on others for its own benefit; if gains must accrue to groups that are radically separate from those that bear costs, it is vital that politically dominant groups bear the costs.

The second purported problem essentially grows out of a quite different concern. Because the legislature does not budget a certain amount of money to be spent on a particular program, it does not adequately assess whether the program is worthwhile.[2] A third, closely related concern is

---

2. This was one of the reasons that traditional opponents of tax expenditures believed the state should collect and expend money directly on desired projects rather than encouraging or funding certain activities by failing to collect the taxes it would ordinarily collect from taxpayers when they spent money in a favored way. For the classic discussion, see Stanley Surrey, "Tax Incentives as a Device for Implementing Government Policy: A Comparison with Direct Government Expenditures," *Harvard L. Rev.* 83 (1970): 705, 728–31. The belief that "implicit" expenditures are not subjected to adequate political scrutiny has also given rise to proposals for Congress to state an explicit regulatory budget in which the costs of private compliance with regulations are listed in the same way that direct expenditures would be. See, e.g., Robert E. Litan and William D. Nordhaus, *Reforming Federal Regulation* (New Haven: Yale University Press, 1983), 133–58; Lance D. Wood, Elliot P. Laws, and Barry Breen, "Restraining the Regulators: Legal Perspectives on a Regulatory Budget for Federal Agencies," *Harvard J. on Legislation* 18 (1981): 1.

This same process concern gave rise to the movement against unfunded mandates, the imposition on states and localities of regulatory directives, which culminated in the passage of the Unfunded Mandates Reform Act of 1995, P.L. 104-4, 109 Stat. 48 (1995) (codified at 2 U.S.C. §§ 658–58g, 1501–71 [Supp. 1995]) (requiring that Congress follow special procedures to enact new unfunded mandates, essentially requiring cost estimates whenever unfunded mandates are proposed, and requiring recorded approval of both houses when states and localities must spend more than fifty million dollars to comply with a federal mandate). For a good description of the law, see, e.g., "Recent Legislation: Federalism—Inter-

that beneficiaries and victims of regulation are simply not clearly known and labeled. At times, critics of regulation offer a particular variant of this argument: regulations too typically mandate that benefits be provided quasi-universally, distributing benefits without the sorts of income qualifications that more tailored spending programs would have. Thus, for example, rent-control subsidizes both rich and poor tenants, though housing vouchers would likely be directed only at the poor.[3] The legislature enacts regulatory programs in a haze, not so much to benefit insiders and discount outsiders but without much sense at all of what is happening.

The legislators may be readily manipulated by the beneficiaries of the regulatory regime and not much dissuaded by its victims (who, for some reason, are either less aware that they are hurt than the beneficiaries know they are helped or are simply less able to exert influence) or may simply operate naively. The ultimate political-process problem, in both cases, is opacity. The legislators never know how much money will be spent (it is the hard-to-estimate sum of private compliance costs) and whether that amount is desirable to spend on that problem rather than on some alter-

---

governmental Relations—Congress Requires a Separate Recorded Vote for Any Provision Establishing an Unfunded Mandate," *Harvard L. Rev.* 103 (1996): 1469. For articles advocating stricter control on such unfunded mandates, see, e.g., Paul Gillmor and Fred Eames, "Reconstruction of Federalism: A Constitutional Amendment to Prohibit Unfunded Mandates," *Harvard. J. on Legislation* 31 (1994): 395; Edward A. Zelinsky, "Unfunded Mandates, Hidden Taxation, and the Tenth Amendment: On Public Choice, Public Interest, and Public Services," *Vanderbilt L. Rev.* 46 (1993): 1355; for articles more skeptical of the attacks on unfunded mandates, see, e.g., David A. Dana, "The Case for Unfunded Environmental Mandates," *Southern California L. Rev.* 69 (1995): 1; Makram B. Jaber, "Unfunded Federal Mandates: An Issue of Federalism or a 'Brilliant Sound Bite,'" *Emory L. J.* 45 (1996): 281.

3. See, e.g., Richard Epstein, "Rent Control and the Theory of Efficient Regulation," *Brooklyn L. Rev.* 54 (1988): 741, 777, 779. Similarly, the minimum wage benefits any employee whose wages are raised by it, even if the employee is part of a well-off family unit. See, e.g., Shaviro, "Minimum Wage," 405, 433–36.

Naturally, there are a number of reasons, including the desire to destigmatize the receipt of government support, to provide at least certain government services more universally rather than limiting them to the poor. For a standard, historical discussion of the tensions between those who believe that welfare should be targeted for efficiency's sake and those who believe that political support for welfare will erode in the absence of greater level of universalization of benefits and that means-tested, more targeted social welfare is unduly stigmatizing, see, e.g., Derek Fraser, *The Evolution of the British Welfare State,* 2d ed. (London: Macmillan, 1984), 194–95, 206–22.

Naturally, too, the goal of certain regulatory programs is less to redistribute by class than to solve some entirely distinct social problem (e.g., rent control may be aimed more at maintaining community continuity or at protecting partial noncommodity relationships with housing than at increasing access to fungible housing services). See Margaret Jane Radin, "Residential Rent Control," *Philosophy and Pub. Affairs* 15 (1986): 350.

native problem (including tax-burden reduction). Moreover, the legislators never identify precisely who is being hurt by a particular amount. Instead of levying a tax whose size and impact on distinct parties is known, parties are told to act without regard to cost. Checks are never sent to particular beneficiaries (and it is never assessed whether they are the ideal recipients), and a funded program whose users are readily identified is never established.

The fourth story is one in which the bureaucratic managers who suggest regulatory options do so because they appear, from a bureaucratic vantage point, free. In one version of this story, a bureaucratic manager is given a quasi-fixed budget and then seeks to maximize influence and power given that budget constraint. In such a world, he will always choose a power-expanding option that does not use up his budget over an alternative that uses up scarce funds, even when that alternative is more effective in meeting the agency's legitimate policy goals. In the other version, the manager is simply cognitively unaware that regulated parties bear costs in the same way that taxpayers who fund the agency's spending programs do. Bureaucrats suffer from fiscal illusion. Believing that off-budget programs are costless or nearly so, the programs inevitably appear to generate more benefits than costs.[4]

It is not clear that these stories are either especially compatible with one another or internally persuasive, though I do not doubt that each has elements of truth. What appears most troubling about the stories, if meant to guide the choice between taxing and spending and regulation, is that they so drastically understate the public-administration problems inherent in the tax-and-spending programs that might substitute for the regulatory mandates and are supposedly superior along these dimensions.

This phenomenon is most obvious when dealing with the purported problem that the benefits and burdens of regulation may so clearly fall on distinct groups that legislation will be driven to too great an extent by the desire to redistribute, rather than meet broader collective goals. It may be the case that pathological tax-and-spending programs seem to be prone to involve transfers from broad taxpayer groups to narrow constituencies and that it is presumed (however naively) that (even disorganized) broad

---

4. For typical arguments to this effect, see, e.g., Blume and Rubinfeld, "Compensation," 569, 620–22; Michelman, "Property, Utility, and Fairness," 1165, 1218; Sax, "Takings," 36, 62–67. For an academic dissent from the mainstream position that fiscal illusion unambiguously leads to excessive, unwarranted government action and that compensation requirements will restrain such action, see Kaplow, "Economic Analysis," 509, 567–70.

groups should be able to protect themselves. (Naturally, though, in standard public-choice models, dispersed majorities are at particular risk of expropriation by well-organized minority groups who care little about aggregate social welfare.) But even if it were believed easier to burden minority groups through regulation than taxation, the pattern of explicit appropriations (on the spending side) may well reflect the devaluation of minority interests. Minorities are just as harmed by broadly financed spending programs that ignore their interests as by taxes that single them out. It is correct to be concerned, for example, that electorally dominant aging baby boomers will impose undue support costs on outvoted Gen Xers by increasing conventional payroll taxes. Even localist pork-barrel legislation may be seen not so much as a series of raids on the fisc by concentrated minority interests exploiting majorities that somehow ought to be able to do better to guard against the theft of their tax money but as majority coalitions of successful pork barrelers exploiting minorities unable to join the dominant coalitions.

Claims that the costs and benefits of regulation are more opaque than those of tax-and-spend programs are also doubtful. Polling evidence, for example, on the popularity of distinct forms of taxation suggests, though it cannot prove, that popular awareness of both the incidence and relative distributive burdens of explicit taxes is low.[5] Moreover, it is doubtful that most legislators recognize that the incidence and distribution of most explicit taxes is contested (whether property taxes, excise taxes, corporate income taxes, or capital gains taxes). Similarly, while it may be obvious how much money a government program basically costs, there are enormous disputes over the net costs of every program and the degree to which beneficiaries other than the most obvious ones really gain. When a municipality funds a sports stadium from an increase in the sales tax, the stadium's costs are transparent, but the level of subsidy to players, team owners, fans, local merchants, and tourist-dependent workers is hotly debated. In fact, some stadium proponents will deny that the stadium has a positive

---

5. Thus, for example, in a 1991 survey, 26 percent of those polled believed that the federal income tax (which is, in fact, mildly progressive) was the least fair tax (including 18 percent of those with incomes under fifteen thousand dollars per year), while only 19 percent thought that state sales taxes (which are, in fact, mildly regressive) were the least fair, including 18 percent of those with incomes under fifteen thousand dollars per year. See *Changing Public Attitudes on Governments and Taxes* (Washington, D.C.: Advisory Commission on Intergovernmental Relations, 1991), 20. In the early 1980s, annual polls revealed that 35 percent or more of those surveyed thought that the federal income tax was the least fair tax, while only 15 percent or fewer thought the state sales tax the least fair. *Id.,* 4.

net cost at all, arguing that increases in sales tax revenues generated by increased visits to the municipality will ultimately make up for initial tax shifts.[6]

At the same time, there are reasons to believe that the costs of regulatory compliance are often clear to legislatures and that these costs, if anything, are overstated by those who will be asked to comply.[7] The idea seems extremely peculiar that actual implicit taxpayers will silently suffer regulation so that legislatures can maintain the belief that regulation is costless. In standard public-choice accounts, concentrated constituencies, like those who bear the costs of regulation, at least at first, are far more likely to note and organize against the imposition of these costs than would dispersed taxpayers facing a small increase in their broad-based taxes.

Similarly, the idea that paying compensation serves to improve government decision making by blunting fiscal illusion seems largely though not wholly unpersuasive for reasons that Rose-Ackerman has highlighted.[8] There appears to be no plausible theory of policy formation in which policymakers would consider the opportunity costs of their proposed actions if and only if they were forced to pay compensation. If they are public-interested cost-benefit calculators, they will account for all costs and benefits regardless of whether they show up in budgets. If policymakers are imperfect agents of the public, they will not be well deterred from improper takings since the expenditures come out of taxpayers' pockets rather than the policymakers' own.[9] If decision making results from the

---

6. For an academic discussion of this issue that concludes that municipalities ultimately subsidize professional sports franchises by building them stadiums, see Dean V. Bain, *The Sports Stadium as a Municipal Investment* (Westport: Greenwood Press, 1994).

7. See Nicholas A. Ashford and Charles C. Caldart, *Technology, Law, and the Working Environment,* 2d ed. (Washington, D.C.: Island Press, 1996), 251–52; U.S. Congress, Office of Technology Assessment, *Gauging Control Technology and Regulating Impacts in Occupational Safety and Health—An Appraisal of OSHA's Analytic Approach* (Washington, D.C., 1995) (postregulatory compliance costs were frequently lower than preregulatory compliance costs as a result of unanticipated technology shifts).

8. Susan Rose-Ackerman, "Against Ad-Hocery: A Comment on Michelman," *Columbia L. Rev.* 88 (1988): 1697, 1706–7. See also, Kaplow, "Economic Analysis of Legal Transitions."

9. Rose-Ackerman's argument here would seem stronger if one assumed that public bureaucrats dominantly seek to maximize the size of the bureaus they govern and that bureau size and budget size are correlated: it is seemingly plausible then that bureaucrats would prefer to increase agency budgets by compensating all owners adversely affected by their programs. But this contention and her more general argument appear no more determinate than the counterclaims made by the proponents of fiscal-illusion theory: to the extent that budgets

conflict of more and less well-organized constituencies, takings law will counteract illusion only if it protects the disorganized whose interests will otherwise be given short shrift. Not only is there little reason to believe that victims of regulation are atypically disorganized in some general sense, one would believe they would be more prone to organize to block regulations than dispersed proponents of regulation would typically organize to seek benefits. In fact, Lunney argues that as a result of the relative ease of organizing those facing concentrated regulatory losses, these owners must be compensated largely to prevent them from blocking socially beneficial regulation, not to prevent socially valueless regulation from coming to pass.[10]

### Rights and Prudence

I believe, although I cannot prove, that there is a distinct political-process problem that typically arises when regulation is chosen rather than tax-and-spend programs.

One of the central antilegalist insights of early critical legal studies (CLS) scholars was that legalism encouraged high levels of reification.[11] When making formal legal arguments or culturally persuasive lay variants of such arguments, lawyers seek to attach a general label to some social situation, attribute features to that particularized social situation typical of situations given the same label, and assert that the consequences that should befall the parties in most similarly labeled situations should also befall them in this particular situation. No one in CLS denied the inevitability of reification—to speak is to reify—but critical scholars simply noted that legalist habits led to more reification than was necessary given linguistic constraints (and that the ability to describe, in language, less reified accounts of the relevant events demonstrated that legalism demanded, or at least seemed to facilitate, higher levels of withdrawal from situation-specific moral discourse than other culturally available

---

are (semi)fixed—taxpayers resist higher taxes, lenders charge more if the governmental entity attempts to borrow more—governmental programs compete with one another. Officials will choose the best programs (however they frame a social, unduly narrowly personal, or interest-group-influenced welfare function) among those competing for budget funds but will always add programs that are (perceived as) costless.

10. See Glynn Lunney, "A Critical Reexamination of Takings Jurisprudence," *Michigan L. Rev.* 90 (1992): 1892, 1947–59.

11. See, e.g., Mark Kelman, *Guide,* 269–75.

forms of discourse). Given that the United States has a highly legalistic culture, though, high levels of reification should be expected.

I believe that the essential image of taxing and spending is that it serves to perform two basic functions: the provision of (loosely defined) public goods and the redistribution of resources (to needy individuals and to interest groups). There are certainly disagreements about these issues: Which goods are truly public? (Is subsidizing education providing a public good? College education? High art? Legal services for the poor?) What are the appropriate levels of spending on concededly public goods? (What is the appropriate size of the [concededly public] defense budget? The appropriate level of air quality, given the costs of attaining higher levels?) Who should be covered by relief for the indigent, and at what levels of support? Should groups, rather than needy individuals, be thought of as apt beneficiaries of public largesse? (Is farmers' income important, regardless of their class status? What about homeowners or tenants in possession? Veterans?) But it is imagined, rather naively, that taxation serves solely to raise funds, as fairly as possible, for general spending programs with standard goals.

Regulation, in the standard reified picture, simply supplements the private law of torts and contracts, insuring that wrongdoers do no harm. Instead of relying on ex post damage judgments to restore parties to the status quo ante in which all entitlements were respected, entitlement breaches are prohibited ex ante. Regulated parties violate rights; beneficiaries are not the objects of redistributive largesse (or consumers of general public goods) but people protected against breaches of entitlement. Zoning and environmental law simply supplement nuisance (and mainstream environmental law casebooks typically first establish the torts/nuisance background for that reason);[12] Title VII brings to the private workplace rights against discriminatory mistreatment; consumer product safety regulations and workplace safety standards supplement product-liability suits and tort suits against employers in a world that disdains assumption-of-risk defenses; sellers' conduct may be regulated in ways that parallel (or mildly expand) buyers' contract rights against fraud (breaches of obligations to engage in appropriate levels of information disclosure), duress, and unconscionability (including undue market power). Regulation, properly done, has liberal priority over taxation and spending; it purifies the

---

12. See, e.g., Frederick R. Anderson, Daniel R. Mandelker, and A. Don Tarlock, *Environmental Protection: Law and Policy,* 2d ed. (Boston: Little, Brown, 1990), 58–65.

private sphere of rights violations, a task to be achieved before redistribution (through taxing and spending).[13]

The problem is that regulations and tax-and-spend programs are alternative means to redistribute and reallocate resources. There may be particular reasons to choose regulation over tax-and-spend programs that have little or nothing to do with protecting the beneficiary class against the violation of its rights. Regulations may be tailored to cause fewer untoward allocative effects than more general taxes that might raise funds sufficient to fund programs generating parallel benefits. Dispersed private parties may be forced by regulation to provide services, uncompensated, because they can do so more cheaply than the state but would not do so if compensated. But in a world that has historically associated the regulatory option with correction of rights violations, there is the tendency to assume that if regulation has occurred, it has been to protect a beneficiary class against a breach of its rights.

Given that rights are ordinarily thought of as (at least partial) side constraints, capable of trumping mere interests or distributive desires, beneficiaries of regulation will not compete directly with redistributive claimants but rather trump their claims. In this view, then, it is a lucky happenstance if distributive claims are best met through regulation, since if they are, it may seem inappropriate either to limit the scope of these claims or to balance them against the distributive claims of competing claimants. In this sense, there is a powerful secondary effect to the fact that as an administrative matter, it is most sensible to implement most programs that aid those with disabilities—whether pupils, consumers, or

---

13. I have no confident moral intuitions about a significant issue implicitly raised in the text: is it proper, in a moral sense, to maintain a substantial sphere (defined by the law of contract, tort, and crime) in which the remediation of rights violations takes priority over alternative forms of welfare-improving state action? Thus, is it morally right that tort plaintiffs have priority over other medically untreated accident victims in claiming the funds that the state charges tort defendants (to deter their malfeasance, as punishment for wrongdoing)? Even trickier, should the state be obliged to take costly, affirmative steps to prevent rights violations by others (e.g., by hiring extra police who might prevent clearly rights-violative crimes) when it could allocate those funds to programs that reduce suffering not caused by what would generally be thought of as rights violations? (If the state could reduce hunger with a food bank program that is cheaper to run than it would be to provide extra police who would reduce violence that is disvalued by its victims no more or less than the hunger the food bank will alleviate, must the state nonetheless first do all it can to reduce crime?)

For purposes of discussing the process defects in using the regulatory option, though, I need simply note two points. First, there is a widespread belief in the priority of remedying, if not preventing, rights violations. Second, this trumping effect may be invoked in situations when rights-violation remedies are employed, even when it is not agreed that the party benefited is really making a persuasive rights claim.

workers—by mandating that dispersed parties meet appropriate accommodation goals: claims that the dollars society allocates to accommodation could be spent meeting the distributive demands of other claimants appear inapt. First, the social world is purified of rights violation—and the cost of remedying (rights violative) discrimination is not a defense—and then redistribution occurs.

I do not want to overstate the impact of using the regulatory option. Classes that have in fact benefited from regulation may well have succeeded in demanding such regulation rather than explicit tax-and-spend programs because the relevant groups were able to convince legislators that their claims were indeed rights-based according to one or another independent theory of entitlements. The theory might well simply be one in which the claimants demonstrated that their situation bore significant similarities to that of other rights claimants. For example, those with disabilities were, like the classic civil rights constituency, African Americans, a socially subordinated distinct and insular minority group with (relatively) immutable traits about whom the majority had serious misconceptions and toward whom it bore animus. The question of whether nonaccommodation was or was not a rights violation may not have turned very much either on whether there was some convincing independent theory that it was (e.g., based on an affirmative right to social inclusion or a distributive right to treatment independent of uncontrollable traits) or on the mere happenstance that the regulation of dispersed public and private parties would be used to benefit the group. Instead, it may have been far more critical that those who sought regulation closely resembled another group that felt it could reach a seemingly parallel goal (social inclusion, an end to involuntary segregation) if classic rights violations (irrational discrimination) were effectively proscribed.

It is clear, though, that however one ultimately evaluates claims that there are substantial affirmative rights to, for example, adequate welfare support levels or reasonable education, efforts to sustain such claims have been at best legally and politically awkward.[14] Conversely, it is scarcely viewed as awkward at all when disability-rights advocates claim as a matter of right that schools must educate children with disabilities appropriately, although schools need not as a matter of right educate anyone else adequately, or that entities must spare no efforts to accommodate those with disabilities unless it becomes pointless to ask entities to do so since

---

14. For the classic, eloquent, yet legally awkward effort to translate affirmative claims on resources into a constitutional right, see Frank I. Michelman, "Welfare Rights in a Constitutional Democracy," *Washington U. L. Q.* (1979): 659.

they will cease to exist as entities if they do. The organized-labor movement's resistance to cost-benefit calculations in worker safety programs[15] may have partially reflected the legitimate fear that these inevitably contentious calculations would take place in an inadequately worker-protective manner or may have reflected a reasonable desire to avoid undue commodification in public discourse.[16] But it is hard to escape the conclusion that no explicitly funded safety program (e.g., a highway construction program in which more or fewer, better or worse barriers might be installed) would ever be enacted without some substantial regard to the costs of saving lives. Conversely, cost-based defenses by employers exposing workers to hazards are strongly disfavored, in part, I suspect, because the employers are simply mandated to cease violating workers' rights.

---

15. Both the AFL-CIO and the Amalgamated Clothing and Textile Workers intervened when the cotton industry unsuccessfully challenged OSHA's cotton-dust regulations. The cotton industry contended that OSHA should not set standards in terms of feasibility but in terms of the regulation's costs and benefits. See *American Textile Manufacturers Institute v. Donovan,* 452 U.S. 490, 493 n. 3 (1981).

16. See Steven Kelman, *What Price Incentives?* (Boston: Auburn House, 1981) 27–83, 95–99, for a discussion of a related phenomenon in relation to environmental quality, the mistrust that some environmentalists and policymakers showed for incentive-based schemes for curtailing pollution. The argument against employing any sort of cost-benefit analysis in relationship to the natural environment is, in a sense, more facially plausible than the argument against employing cost-benefit thinking in the health and safety context. In the environmental context, it is not obvious that humans should act as though as they are entitled to alter the natural world whenever it is worth more to them to do so than it deserves their own interests. In relationship to their own health or safety, though, there are significant prudential arguments against collective cost-benefit analysis—that risks may be imposed by some on others, for example—but it appears difficult to argue seriously that individuals ought never balance the benefits of decreased risk or increased expected longevity against other improvements in life quality. See Richard Abel, "A Socialist Approach to Risk," *Maryland L. Rev.* 41 (1982): 695 (noting that both market and political decisions about risk allocation at work and in consumption may be problematic in class societies while recognizing that individuals may reasonably balance the costs and benefits of risky activities in ideal settings, some of which exist in certain domains).

# CHAPTER 6

## Conclusion

There are, in my view, no constitutional principles that would regularly force governmental entities to use tax-and-spend programs rather than regulatory ones. (Courts should also never order these entities to let losses lie rather than remedy or prevent some harm or to employ user fees or benefits taxes, even though there are situations in which some observers might well be able to make a good case that these solutions to social problems are more appropriate.) Even if Justice Scalia is correct to believe that it is possible to distinguish situations that involve "pure" regulation (the reduction or allocation of social costs or the policing of unjust contracts) from those in which regulation substitutes for a traditional tax-and-spend program, analysis of the suspect regulations as disguised tax-and-spend programs shows that they almost invariably withstand constitutional scrutiny.

Regulations may indeed substitute for available tax-and-spend programs (and the reverse is true as well), but if the suspect regulations are analyzed as implicit taxes followed by implicit spending programs, there is generally no good basis for the Court to intervene to undo either the implicit tax or the implicit spending programs. Virtually no regulatory taxes violate the justifiably slim equal-protection principles against unduly narrowly based taxation, and no regulatory spending programs violate the even more trivial constitutional limits on narrowly focused benefits. It is remotely conceivable that a court might strike down a particular regulatory tax because it required particularistic knowledge of a taxpayer that could only be gained through undue intrusion in the implicit taxpayer's affairs, but it is hard to imagine realistic cases in which existing regulations would fail on that ground.

The prudential limits on the use of regulation are far harder to summarize but ultimately considerably more significant than the constitutional ones. In assessing which form of government action to employ, it is necessary to try to answer a number of questions on the tax side: How will the implicit tax impact behavior, given the desire to minimize undue allocative dislocation? How expensive will the tax be to administer compared to available alternatives? Will it result in a fair distribution of burdens, given certain conceptions of posttax distributive justice (vertical equity, properly understood)? How will the tax meet the substantive concerns often mischaracterized as horizontal equity concerns: maintenance of allocative incentives; avoidance of status-based discrimination; reduction in rent seeking; and minimization of privacy intrusions.

Opponents of regulatory taxation have not only underestimated the possible tax advantages of regulation but also wholly failed to focus on its spending-side advantages. It is dangerous to overstate the inevitable cost-effectiveness or innovativeness of private entities—this is, after all, a country that enjoys its most marked technical superiority in the three industries (agriculture, computers, and aerospace) most dominated by government research and development—but there are certainly situations in which dispersed private producers will both know more about how to deliver desired services than will the state and operate with superior incentives to reduce costs. Compensating these private producers for the cost of actual service provision may frequently blunt whatever desirable incentives they would otherwise face, and compensating for typical costs may lead producers to devote a good deal more resources to winning the political battle over how much they should receive than to minimizing service-provision costs. These problems will be less severe when the regulated entity can meet the state's goal only by forbearing from conduct entirely, but in many cases in which the government has simply enacted restrictive regulations, it is possible to meet regulatory goals either through remedial action that offsets the initial ill effects of conduct or through forbearance, so that maintenance of incentives for cost-effective remedial action is desirable.

It might well be that governmental entities have enacted regulations that unduly burden disenfranchised subgroups, but there is no guarantee that tax-and-spend programs will do a better job protecting either disorganized majorities or outvoted minorities. The total costs (and distribution of the costs) of regulation may indeed sometimes be opaque, but this, too, is a problem in explicit taxing and spending. I believe, however, that the political process may indeed be distorted when regulations are used instead of taxing and spending to the degree that it is socially plausible that regulation's beneficiaries make entitlement-based rather than redistributive claims and that their claims therefore trump those made by beneficiaries of the welfare state.

# Index

accommodations, 7–8, 51, 103n. 58, 106, 114, 122–23; defining reasonableness of accommodation, 56, 98; as implicit taxes, 92–93; misperceptions of costs, 8, 81; retrofitting v. prospective accommodations, 8, 52–53, 55

Ackerman, Bruce, 14n. 16, 19

administrative costs, 36–37, 39, 67–68, 77, 94–95, 109, 110–12, 126

allocative efficiency, 76–77, 99, 122, 125–26

Americans with Disabilities Act (ADA), 7–9, 86; constitutional considerations, 16n. 19, 17, 22, 25–27, 29, 31–32, 40–41, 50–56, 68; as implicit spending program, 103n. 58, 106, 108–9; as implicit tax on those providing accommodations, 92–93

antidiscrimination norms, 8–9, 100, 121, 123

benefit taxes, 50, 70, 77, 79, 98–99

bureaucratic self-interest, 78–79, 113, 117

causation of harm, 48–50, 54

Coase, Ronald, 48–49, 53, 84n. 17

cost and cost-plus procurement, 77, 107–12, 126

deadweight loss, 65, 93, 111

deliberate government inaction, 4–5, 70, 75–76, 77, 79, 81–84, 102

disemployment effects, 82–83, 85–87

*Dolan v. City of Tigard,* 12n. 11, 16–17, 26, 32–33, 35–40, 49–50, 52–54, 55, 60, 65, 67–70

economic rents, 57–59, 66–67, 80–81n. 11, 87–88, 91–92

Epstein, Richard, 11, 14n. 16, 116n. 3

Equal Protection and taxation, 60–63, 100–101, 125

exactions, 50, 61; constitutional considerations, 16–17, 32–41; as optimal taxes, 66, 86–88

exploitation of contractual partners, 10n. 8, 12–13, 24–25, 45–48, 69

fair distribution of tax burdens, 64n. 37, 65n. 38, 67n. 42, 96–103, 126

fiscal illusion, 102n. 54, 113, 117, 119–20

*Hall v. City of Santa Barbara,* 13n. 15, 43n. 2, 56–59

*Hawaii Housing Authority v. Midkiff,* 18n. 23, 58–59

*Heart of Atlanta Motel, Inc. v. United States,* 20n. 30, 25n. 44, 26

*Hodel v. Irving,* 20n. 29, 23, 37

horizontal equity, 64n. 37, 77, 99–103, 126

implicit spending programs, 13n. 15; effectiveness of private delegate, 77–78, 105–6, 108–9; 'public' v. 'private' beneficiaries 43, 46, 56–59, 122

127